CW00685598

A TALE OF TWO RIVERS

MAWDDACH and DYFI
and the land between
CADAIR IDRIS

PHOTOGRAPHS
JEAN NAPIER

TEXT
ALUN JOHN RICHARDS

Dedicated to all who love
the culture and beauty of Wales

First published: 2005
Second edition: 2007

© Text: Alun John Richards; Photographs: Jean Napier

Copyright © by Gwasg Carreg Gwalch 2005.

All rights reserved. No part of this publication
may be reproduced or transmitted, in any form
or by any means, without permission.

ISBN: 0-86381-989-3

Published by
Gwasg Carreg Gwalch,
12 Iard yr Orsaf, Llanrwst, Wales, LL26 0EH.
Tel: 01492 642031 Fax: 01492 641502
e-mail: llyfrau@carreg-gwalch.co.uk
www.carreg-gwalch.co.uk

Printed and published in Wales.

A Meeting of Minds

They could not be more dissimilar, one male one female, you cannot get much more different than that for starters.

Separated more by a generation chasm than a generation gap. One Welsh, one east London English, one with a head in the past, one with eyes to the future.

One firmly espoused to the word-processor, one to the camera. Admittedly both were once professional engineers but one was in the heavy "smokestack" end, the other in automotive production.

Holding diverse opinions on almost every subject, with no discernable meeting of minds whatsoever - except an appreciation of Wales, its culture and its slate and indeed an admiration of each other's work.

Meeting at Plas Tan y Bwlch, that crucible of many a seminal project, he felt as honoured to be asked to write a foreword to her then forthcoming book, as she was to his agreeing to do so.

During the ensuing acquaintanceship, a mutual feeling grew that they could combine talents. This culminated in a meeting in a Machynlleth hotel where it was agreed that their shared fascination with the changing moods of rivers as they journey from birthplace to death or metamorphosis in the sea, should be the basis of this book.

There followed over three years of work. Jean walking many miles up and down mountains and valleys seeking the locations that best expressed her emotions about the rivers, returning, sometimes repeatedly, to capture the exact combination of season, light, weather and tide.

Alun, researching file and archive, interviewing his and Jean's contacts, chasing myth and fact, and always the endless fieldwork trudge, ensuring that not even the cranniest nook remained unvisited.

PREVIOUS BOOKS

Jean Napier

Rhosydd A Personal View – Golwg Bersonol	IBSN0-86381-470-0

Alun John Richards

A Gazeteer of the Welsh Slate Industry	IBSN 0-86381-196-5
Slate Quarrying at Corris	IBSN 0-86381-279-1
Slate Quarrying in Wales	IBSN 0-86381-319-4
Slate Quarrying in Pembrokeshire	IBSN 0-86381-484-0
The Slate Regions of North& Mid Wales	IBSN 0-86381-552-9
The Slate Railways of Wales	IBSN 0-86381-689-4
Fragments of Mine and Mill	IBSN 0-86381-812-9
(With Gwynfor Pierce Jones)	
Cwm Gwyrfai	IBSN 0-86381-987-8

All published by Gwasg Carreg Gwalch

Jean Napier ARPS

Born in East London, Jean Napier has lived in the Snowdonia National Park since 1991 and the magnificent scenery is the main inspiration for her photography. Man's influences on the landscape of Wales are a recurring theme in her exhibitions and photography books and her first book "Rhosydd – A Personal View" depicts the remains of an old slate quarry in northern Wales with historical text and is bilingual.

Her primary motivation is to promote photography as an art form, to show the versatility and creativity of the photographic image; that it is not just a method of 'recording' moments. Her work has been exhibited throughout the UK, in the USA and Australia.

She teaches photography to a variety of students of all ages and levels throughout the UK and is a tutor and assessor for the Open College of Art. She holds a BA Honours Degree in Photographic Studies and is an Associate of the Royal Photographic Society.

Further information and a gallery are available on www.jean-napier.com

Alun John Richards

A retired engineer who for many years was a guest tutor at the Snowdonia National Park Environmental Studies Centre, Plas Tan y Bwlch and sometime lecturer at Coleg Harlech Summer Schools.

A native of Swansea he is a past Chairman of the South West Wales Industrial Archaeology Society and of the Swansea Art Society

Although his speciality is the Welsh slate industry on which he is an acknowledged expert, he also writes and lectures on a variety of aspects of industrial history.

He is also a vigorous defender of the landscape and environment of Wales

www.richards-slate.co.uk

Rhwngyddwyafon – Between Two Rivers

"The rivers of Wales," I was told decades ago by an old fisherman in a kind of pothouse or turf-tavern in Eifionydd (he and it and both their kind long gone, to the detriment of the entire nation), "are like its women – short and turbulent and exceedingly beautiful, especially in their youth". He was one of those *hen gymeiriadau* worthy of the pen of a D J Williams, who had cast in his time a fly in every deep and trout-stippled pool from the Teifi to the Saint, whilst observing there in wry detachment all the riparian eccentricities of man and woman and nature itself. No Calvinist, names to him were a joyful litany, to be rehearsed as list of contents to the narrative of a fulfilled life. I can hear him chanting them out now, face creased with memory's laughter: "Dwyfor, Dwyryd, Dyfrdwy, Dyfi, Artro, Angell, Mynach, Mawddach".

In this volume the photographer Jean Napier and slate historian Alun John Richards have followed the courses of two of them – Mawddach and Dyfi – from source to sea, evoking story and mood of landscape as they go. The rivers rise a raven's glide apart in Penllyn and flow in parallel to Bae Ceredigion. From the magnificent desolation of Waun y Griafolen down to the bird-haunted foreshores of Ynys-las, the land they encompass, in all its natural loveliness and human record, is as entrancing as any in our jewelled nation. This book will help you come to know it better, and hence to love it all the more.

Jim Perrin, Hiraethog, Ionawr 2005

Introduction

When considering rivers with both banks exclusively Welsh, many have claims to fame. The majesty of Afon Conwy, the haunting beauty of Dwyfor, the cascades of Afon Mellte or the white water cataracts of Tryweryn, there are a score or more candidates.

However for a combination of all the attributes, the joint sovereigns regnant, the king and queen of all the rivers must be Afon Mawddach and Afon Dyfi. They of course have a head start on other contenders in that they are in Meirionnydd, where the terrain was once described as - "The rudest and ruggedest in all Wales, the ridges of its mountains high and narrow terminating in rough peaks."

This landscape is moulded by its underlying Cambrian rock that in earlier times when earth science was less well understood, was believed to be the oldest geological series. It was therefore argued that Meirionnydd must have been the first part of the world that the Almighty created and having no other pattern to draw upon, He modelled it on heaven itself. It is said that the Angels prevailed upon the Almighty to make the rest of the earth to a lesser standard lest people would feel no wish to go to heaven.

The two rivers have similarities, they follow parallel courses, they each have a seaport on the northern extremity of their estuaries and a market town adjacent to their lowest bridge-points. They each had similar traditions of trade and of extractive industries and in the course of their journey to the sea, each has three distinct phases; mountain, sedate rural and navigable estuary.

However, directly one abandons the atlas, the dissimilarities become manifest.

The Mawddach rises unobtrusively but shortly becomes a formidable force even before gathering its tributaries, whereas the infant Dyfi comprises several small but very overt torrents.

The mature Mawddach is short and can never escape its gorge-like propensities whereas the Dyfi is longer with broader banks.

Where they become estuarial the differences are even more marked. Below the bridge point the Mawddach immediately transforms into a beauty that can stand world comparison but the lower Dyfi cannot shake off its middle-river image, meandering until its banks diverge so abruptly as to create a seascape rather than a river vista.

Contents

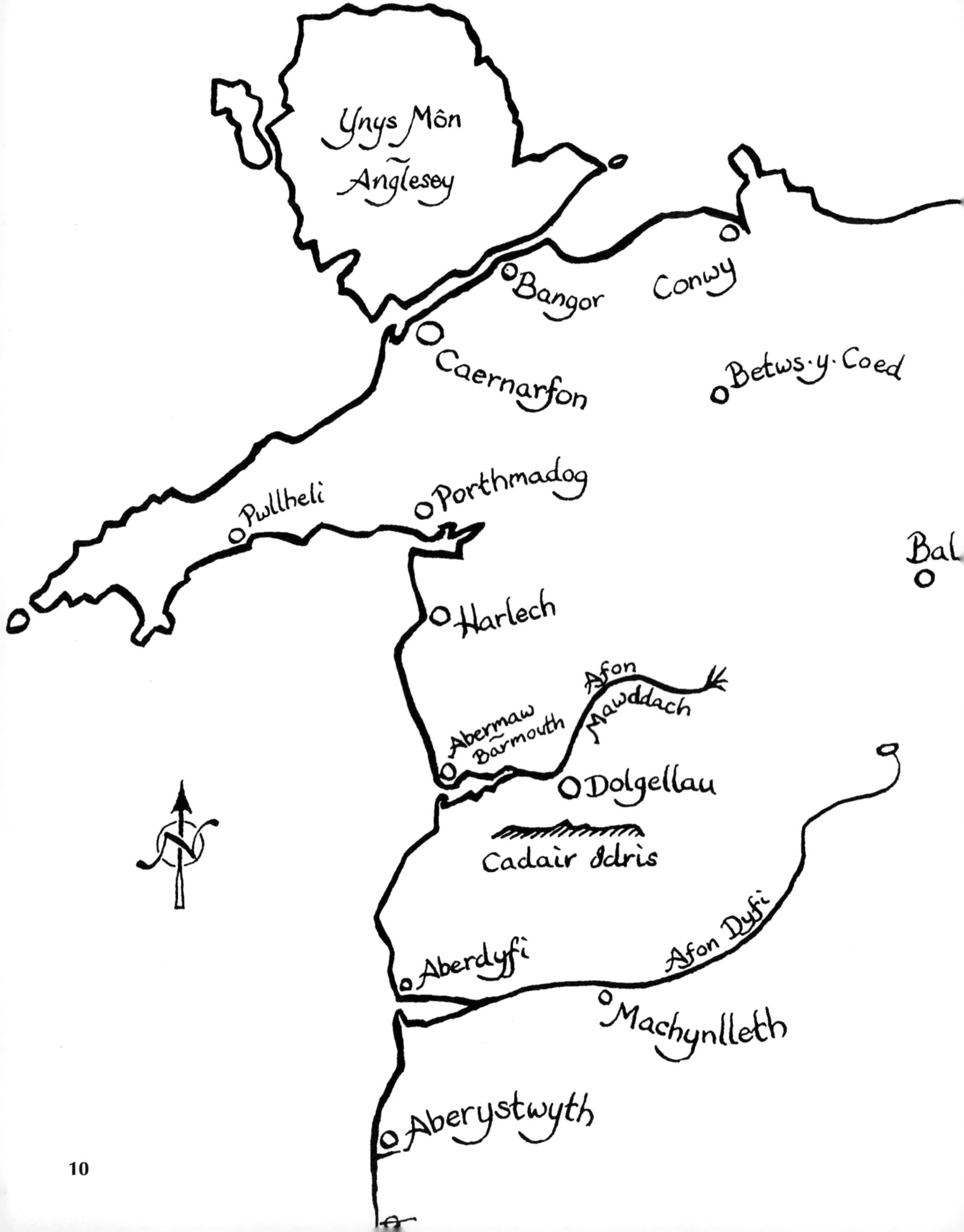

Ynys Môn
Anglesey

○ Bangor   Conwy

○ Caernarfon   ○ Betws-y-Coed

○ Pwllheli   ○ Porthmadog   Bal

○ Harlech

Afon
Mawddach

Abermaw
Barmouth

○ Dolgellau

Cadair Idris

Aberdyfi   Afon Dyfi

○ Machynlleth

Aberystwyth

MAWDDACH

Afon Mawddach

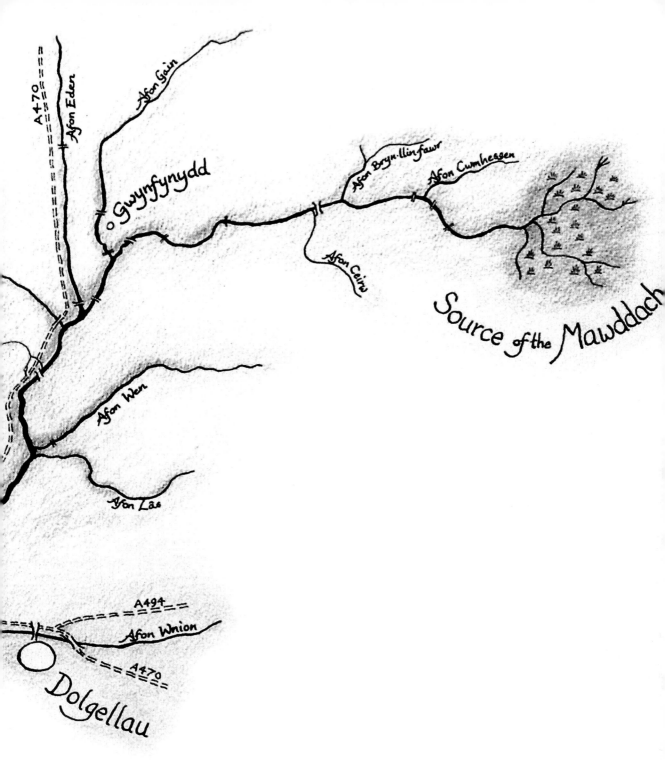

MAWDDACH
1
THE SOURCE

The desolate and unprepossessing upland waste where the Mawddach rises in remote obscurity gives no hint of its later glories where, using new-found muscles, it gouges a spectacular gorge unique to Wales and goes on to produce an estuarial vista of unparalleled splendour.

First it must assemble itself and its moist oozings must decide whether to throw in their lot with the Afon Lliw and seek an eastward, half English destiny, or to remain true their Meirionnydd roots and join the rivulets and rills that mark the land, like veins on an aged hand, as they hesitantly gravitate towards the Cwm yr Alltlwyd to form a bona-fide mountain stream. Here in what was once described as a *"belt of unremitting poverty"*, in an ethos equally hostile to man and beast life was, and still is, hard and primitive. Here the relentless rain can sluice the life from a newborn lamb before it can seek the ewe's teat.

Even wildlife is scarce, the white eagle, with its great barn-door wings that made a sparrow of its golden cousin, has been gone for half a millennium. In the 19th century, when the gentry started to shoot pheasants rather than peasants, their keepers slaughtered everything that might harm their precious partridges. peregrines, hen harriers, merlins and sparrow hawks were relentlessly hunted; even the now-nurtured kites did not escape their assiduous attentions as they strove to maximise their knickerbockered masters' sport.

The stream's first encounter with human habitation was at the now deserted farms, Dôl Cyn Afon and Allt Lwyd, glowering at each other across the infant river. In 1833 Gruffydd Jones of Allt Lwyd found William Jones of Dôl Cyn Afon lurking in an outbuilding and clearly up to no good. Accordingly, Jones (G) demanded "satisfaction" from Jones (W).

Legend has it that the two Jones', accompanied by their respective trio of sons, battled with scythes and that so much blood was spilled that the river ran red, but the truth of this regrettable affair is more prosaic.

Since most of the adult male population of this part of the valley was eventually called as witnesses and the conflict took place at nearby Rhiwfelen farm, it was clearly a fixture pre-arranged on neutral ground. The three sons from each family met at 7.00 a.m. on the 11th of October to champion their respective fathers' honour in what was apparently a bare-knuckled melee. Being a Friday it was clearly timed to take place prior to everyone going to Dolgellau market.

When Rhys Jones, a son of Allt Lwyd, was downed obviously suffering serious hurt, onlookers intervened and a horseman was dispatched to Dolgellau to fetch a doctor who arrived to find that the unfortunate Rhys was dead. As a consequence, both fathers and the five surviving sons all found themselves guests of King William at Dolgellau gaol and were ultimately brought before the dreaded Red Judge of Assize. Charges against both fathers and the deceased's two brothers were dropped, two of the Dôl Cyn Afon sons were found not guilty, leaving their brother John Williams, to "carry the can" (the custom of a son using his father's Christian name as a patronymic was still often followed).

The court found that -

"-not having the fear of God before his eyes but being moved and seduced by the instigation of the Devil - [he did] feloniously wilfully and unlawfully —strike and beat — the said Rhys Jones [committing] the Foul Deed of Manslaughter."

Strong words indeed, but the judge seems to have taken the view that with no sheep-stealing or poaching involved, no great harm had been done and sentenced Williams to two months in Dolgellau gaol. This was of course served in the "new" gaol (on the site of the present Council Offices) which, though primitive by our standards, was a holiday camp compared with the hellhole of an oubliette that it had recently replaced.

A little below at Abergeirw is a bridge; such bridges located far from what we would call the beaten track were of vital importance. Cattle could wade a small stream, or swim a full-scale river, but a fast flowing mountain torrent defeated them, and thus these remote bridges were essential to drovers. One supposes that as these *porthmwyn* Bala-bound from Harlech braved mud and tempest, rogues and robbers, whilst harrying their beasts and urging their dogs, they would have been oblivious of the world of banking and finance that their activities would create. Droving is widely assumed to have been for beef cattle raised around the periphery of Bae Ceredigion (*Cardigan Bay*), but actually a proportion would have been draught oxen as well as milking stock for the numerous Welsh-owned dairies in London and elsewhere. Some beasts would have been shipped from Ireland and cattle drovers also handled other livestock such sheep, pigs and geese.

Roads were of course shunned, green track ways gave easier walking for the animals and, after turnpikes appeared in the 18th century, their dreaded tollhouses had to be circumvented.

Adjacent to the Abergeirw Bridge is a Methodist chapel built at a time when a Dissenter was lucky to escape with his life if he fell into the clutches of an Anglican squire. Solitarily sited to elude the purview of the Archdeacon of Meirionnydd, and of architecturally anonymous aspect so that if that Venerable clerk should happen to stumble upon it, its purpose might not be immediately apparent.

The presence of this unpretentious but godly edifice causes the stream to scurry past like a Devil's familiar seeking the safety of the nether regions. As the waters tumble and twist, the sides of the savage canyon they create provide precarious footholds for ancient broadleaf trees that have somehow evaded the charcoal burner, the shipbuilder and the river's savage spates. These woods, clinging to the gorge flanks, remnants of vast forested tracts, have survived unchanged for millennia. They offer shelter from the moorland winds of winter to day-shy badgers, ethereal goats, and grey squirrels gloating over their vanquishment of the red. The wolves and wildcats have long gone, but a few otters have survived slaughter by keepers and hunters, leaving the foxes and the mink to terrorise the rabbits, the voles and regrettably, the sheep. The voles and their kind also are prey to the short-eared owls that like the lesser red poll thrive in the Sitka spruce.

The fox as a pest is nothing new. Under a 1566 Act of Queen Elizabeth, churchwardens were obliged to maintain a fund to enable them to pay 12 pence (more than £12 today) for the head of every fox. A hundred years later five times as much was being paid out and by the early 19th century anything up to £1 was on offer which, at the time, was at least a couple of month's pay for a live-in labourer. No wonder precautions had to be taken to *"Avoyde fraude and deceit in the killer of any of the sd vermines, in bringing the sayd vermine twice"*.

The deep defiles have given rise to a number of "leap legends", usually involving a witch turning into a stag, enabling her to not only outrun her pursuers, but to jump a gap leading them, their mounts and their dogs to plunge lemming-like to destruction.

There being more witches than you could shake a broomstick at, called for the provision of "witches seats", stone projections on chimney or church to discourage such ladies from seeking respite inside the building. Whilst we now attribute natural calamity not so much to witches as to global warming or the EEC, there still lurks a redolence of sorcery in these shadowed chasms. A nocturnal encounter with the evilly mischievous *Tylwyth Teg* (Fairies) or the fearsome *Ceffyl Dwfr* (Water Horse), or that monstrous mastiff the *Gwyllgi*, is still regarded as bordering on the realms of possibility.

Both the *Cannwyl Gorff* (Corpse candle) and the *Olwyn Dân* (Fiery Wheel) have been seen on the Mawddach lighting the way for the Angel of Death hurrying to his next assignment. There are tales almost within living memory of the frightful, *Aderyn Corff* (Corpse Bird) assuming commonplace avian guise and dashing itself to death against a window then demanding a human life in place of its own.

Confident in its own immortality, the Mawddach allies itself with the great cascades of the Afon Cain and surges down the ravine with redoubled vigour, a gentle roar proclaiming its benevolent authority. Yet just occasionally it would seem that these forces of darkness cause it to rail against the confines of its gorge like a captive beast hysterically hurling itself at the bars of its cage.

Paradoxically it was this same unreasoning anger, so terrifyingly displayed in 2001 when a dozen bridges were destroyed or fatally damaged, that first exposed the minerals that made fortunes by the dozen and lost them by the score.

Initially it was copper; the metal that combined with the tin of Cornwall made the proto-industry of the Bronze Age. But it was in the secret reaches of the upper Mawddach, when the young Victoria was newly crowned, that copper miners realised the true identity of the glistening substance adulterating their ores, triggering a stampede of gold-driven greed.

Reluctantly leaving its gorge near Ganllwyd, the Mawddach is joined by the Eden. Unlike its previous alliance with the Gain that provoked it to greater intensities, the Eden persuades the Mawddach to proceed with a more measured pace appropriate to a newfound dignity which not even confluence with the flighty Afon Gamlan and thrusting Afon Wen can disturb.

This is the territory of the pine trees in all their guises, Coed y Brenin, that vast strategic reserve of poles, planks and pit props that provides a coniferous echo of the frantic oak-plantings for the ships of Nelson and Drake. Such plantations provide scant habitat for native fauna and flora, but neither do they harbour the foul phantoms of the ancient woods.

The village of Ganllwyd itself is dominated by the Dolymelynllyn estate noted for its lush pasture and the production of the honey so prized in pre-sugar times and once the home of W.A. Maddocks the "inventor" of Tremadog and Porthmadog. It was when living here at the turn of 18th/19th centuries that Maddocks unsuccessfully tried to create interest in the exploitation of manganese in the county, possibly seeing a market for it in the local woollen industry for bleaching purposes.

The trim parkland of the estate makes a fitting setting for the Mawddach's emergence into the wider world enjoying for a few miles its distinction of being the only significant Welsh valley never to have been sullied by a locomotive.

MAWDDACH
2
GWYNFYNYDD GOLD MINE

Although there are apocryphal tales of a 17th century Mr.Bushel *"Having a gold mine near Dolgeley"*, the first proven find was in 1844 when miners seeking copper where the Heisian brook is swallowed by the Mawddach made the sensational discovery that the adage *"All that glisters is not gold"* is not always true. This created a fever of excavation on what became known as the Dolgellau "Gold Belt". Throughout the latter half of the 19th century, anywhere from the coast to Bala and Trawsfynydd, rags could turn to riches as quickly as the reverse could occur.

Actually, as was confirmed in 1833 by the discovery of a bronze age gold cape at Mold, gold had been worked in Wales some three millennia earlier. The workmanship of this artefact has been likened to that of the gold items later found at Troy by Heinrich Schliemann, and in fact it has been claimed that the craftsmanship far from being brought to Wales by the Celts, may have been developed in Wales and passed eastwards.

Either way not only the skill but also the origin of the gold was lost. The Romans, so efficient in resource exploitation as was shown by their specialist army engineers in the south Wales gold mines, failed to find the Mawddach deposits.

Gold, apart from its appearance and resistance to tarnishing, has always been prized since it is easy to work with basic tools, but more importantly occurs as a metal that does not require smelting. Unfortunately, unlike most other minerals it does not occur in identifiable and predictable veins. Geologists can say with certainly where gold will not be found, but can only express probability as to where it might be found.

Alluvial gold, where classically the old bearded prospector squats jiggling his pan, is a rarity in Wales although some streams hereabouts were optimistically panned in the 18th century. (Modern "tourist" panning generally depends on the tailings from mining spoil.)

In Wales gold is invariably locked into unyielding rock deep underground from where it has to be sought, blasted, pulverised, converted to slurry and painstakingly separated, concentrated and amalgamated in complex machines, not so much pinhead by pinhead as pinpoint by pinpoint.

Unfortunately gold, like a trollop raising a skirt to afford a tantalising glimpse of a bejewelled garter, can manifest itself as rich pockets, assaying not as ounces but as hundreds of ounces Troy per ton, seducing prospectors to extrapolate samplings into untold riches. Invariably such dreams prove as false, as expensive and as fleeting as a whore's charms, and there are countless instances of infrastructure being installed and machinery being bought to process an expected bonanza only to have the deposit vanish as mysteriously and abruptly as it appeared.

Consequently only a third of the almost 70 mines in Meirionnydd ever produced marketable metal and perhaps as few as 2 were more than briefly and marginally profitable.

Here, high in the secret reaches of the Mawddach valley, directly opposite the ruins of Cwm Heisian mine where it all began, are the remnants of Gwynfynydd gold mine, now sadly savaged by the great storm of 2001. Here in 1864 the lead miners discovered that the gold manifest across the river at Heisian was also present on their patch.

Although Gwynfynydd is commonly associated with the great 1860s "Dolgellau Gold Rush", this was centred on the northern flank of the river downstream of Dolgellau. Gwynfynydd produced almost no gold until the early 1880s, it only really came into its own when that prince of mine captains; ex-barrister, ex-Antipodean speculator Pritchard Morgan, who treated practical difficulties with as much distain as he treated

legal ones, took charge in 1887. In the following never-to-be-repeated year, he raised more than a quarter of a ton of gold.

He immediately arranged for two police constables to guard the mine. Their effectiveness as discouragers of pilferage may have been questionable, but their effectiveness as encouragers of investment was undoubted, promoting a very warm perception of riches to potential shareholders. Morgan's ability to extract gold from the rock being more than matched by his ability to extract money from speculators and doubtless he also had publicity in mind when he famously used the door of the old Dolgellau gaol for his strong room.

Before long some 200 miners honeycombed the hillside with their tunnels, winzes and stopes, tapping the great Barlow lode. Many more worked in the mill a little way downstream where the great waterwheel, backed up by a 120hp steam engine, ground and stamped and pulverised the ore as inexorably as the Mills of God.

Following the installation of stamps imported from the USA, some Americans were employed; this not only

reversed migration patterns, but defied the belief that - *Nid yw'r creigiau deall Saeseneg* (the rocks don't understand English), it being widely held that the ground was readier to yield its riches if hard graft was accompanied by verbal blandishments in the native tongue. A saying that undoubtedly arises from the fact that an experienced local miner could recognise a gold bearing pocket more readily that a stranger.

Some of the workmen walked considerable distances daily, others lodged with farmers contributing work in summer evenings in part-payment for their keep, but many slept in the barracks during the week. Dolgellau barrackers would meet at the town bridge at 3.00 on a Monday morning to commence the 8½ mile walk. Carrying their wallets on across a shoulder, one side holding a loaf of bread and the other provisions for the week, they would take a rest at Ty'n y Groes and another at Tyddyn Gwladys arriving at the mine for a 6 a.m. start.

The food the miners brought with them could be augmented by the mid-week pony and trap delivery by the grocers Messrs Miles and Williams of Dolgellau,

but more usually they relied on whatever they could catch, invariably rabbits, giving rise to the ditty

Rabbits young, rabbits old
Rabbits hot, rabbits cold
Rabbits tender, rabbits tough
Thank the Lord, we had enough.
Attributed to Hugh Pugh, of Dolgellau. Mill Foreman at Gwynfynydd, but probably not original

It was at Tyddyn Gwladys that in 1860 a Mr Roberts of Dolgellau employed two men to prospect for lead. Tiring of such a vain task one fell asleep, but on awakening tripped on a boulder which, in a temper, he smashed with his pick revealing the sought-for lead ore. Later both silver and gold were found but yields of metals of any kind were disappointing as were those of all the upper Mawddach diggings with the exception of Gwynfnydd. Thus in 1887 the mine machinery was turned to the making of gunpowder to supply their more metallurgically blessed neighbours.

By the early 1890s the works were disused and had been taken over by Morgan, who having established that revival of mining there was not on, made use of the buildings as a barracks and reading room where, amongst other "improving activities", Bible classes were held. The real reason for the takeover was to obtain Afon Cain water rights, enabling the Gwynfynydd mill to be upgraded and driven by a powerful water-turbine fed by the combined rivers. He was also able to utilise Tyddyn land to build a much-improved access road. He included in the tramway layout a self-acting balanced incline, commonplace in slate and stone workings but very much a rarity in Welsh metal mining.

For a time Morgan was Liberal MP for Merthyr Tydfil, being eventually ousted by Kier Hardie the first Labour member. To boost his benefactor image, Morgan presented a gold baton to be competed for at the National Eisteddfod, but gold and greed begin with the same initial letter so a serious rift and even litigation rocked choral circles. The lawsuit was quickly disposed of, but the rancour lasted a generation.

By the mid 1890s the rock quality was declining and becoming more elusive so in 1901 Morgan wisely sold out just ahead of the early 20th century market stagnation.

Production fell and by the outbreak of WW1 Gwynfynydd was history and in 1915 the mill machinery was scrapped and the lathes and so on from the well-equipped repair shop were reinstalled in a shell factory at Ruabon.

In the ensuing years, millions have been spent vainly trying to emulate the Morgan magic. Certainly in the 1980s some gold was produced but a fall in prices and unexpected geological difficulties brought serious losses. In the 1990s it operated at as tourist attraction.

Regrettably, although the 2001 flood did not affect the actual workings, the destruction it wrought above ground pushes even higher the level of gold prices that would be required to justify reopening.

Copper was mined hereabouts with varying success, in fact several copper mines produced gold and silver as a minor sideline. This was the case at Glasdir mine on whose terraces in the early 1900s, the Manager Stanley Elmore developed his eponymous floatation process that became the worldwide standard method of precious metal ore separation. There are extensive surface remains of the foundations for the stamps, crushers

and vestiges of the buddles and settling tanks. Notable are the wooden casks in which Elmore's chemicals were delivered.

Some gold was obtained at the nearby and very ancient Dolfrwynog copper mine but Dofrwynog's claim to fame was its peat which was so copper-rich that it could be dug and burnt on the spot leaving ash that could be bagged and carted to Dolgellau for sale to the Swansea smelters.

Anyway, all this activity had its downside, in 1898 Arthur Bradley wrote. *"There is a copper mine (Glasdir) which enjoys the unusual distinction of having polluted one of the most pellucid and romantic rivers in North Wales, the only one too, that I know in all this country which has been so abused, for the once bright Mawddach now goes leaping down its winding glen from Tyn-y-groes to Cymer, a torrent of thick milk."*

Tests showed that the effluent was harmless although paradoxically a 15hp hydroelectric plant installed in 1930 to light Llanfachreth village did cause problems due to the release of contaminated water from the old workings. This pollution controversy re-appeared at Gwynfynydd during one of its late 20th century revivals.

Now with industry gone, the river runs crystal-clear but the regulations which ensure the continuance of this may well make it economically impracticable to revive metallic extraction, particularly as modern methods can involve noxious chemicals such as cyanide.

MAWDDACH
3
LLANELLTYD

Hauntingly sited on the slopes of Y Garn, high above the river as it moves towards Llanelltyd, are small gold diggings where handfuls of men endlessly toiled, sustained by their optimism that they would one day find themselves at the centre of a California-like bonanza. Except for their lack of metal any one of them might be the prototype for Mr. Dinwiddy, Ivor the Engine's gold mining friend.

A little lower down the river at Dôl y Clochrhyd a charcoal ironworks was opened in the mid 16th century on land expropriated from the monks of Cymer. It was let by Hugh Nanney in 1588 to two English "adventurers", John Smith of Newcastle-under-Lyme and William Dale a London Grocer, who were prepared to set up at what they called *"the fag end of creation"* to supply the Grosvenor forges at Chester, then furiously making arms to subdue the Irish.

When they expressed concern about a source of timber, Nanney allegedly said "No problem" and guaranteed an ample supply from Penrose Common. Unfortunately this was Crown property, and Nanney was High Sheriff, effectively the Crown's local rep! It was 1604 before King James found out about it; by which time 30,000 of his prime oak trees nurtured for the navy had been felled and furnaced. His reaction being somewhat short of delight, he fined Nanney the equivalent of £125,000 and banged him up in the Fleet Prison for 2 years.

This site found a re-use in the early 20th century when a small, waterwheel-driven buddle was built to sift the water leaching from an abandoned trial on the hillside above. Its arm slowly rotated day in day out, year in year out settling out the slimes, in the vain hope that one day particles of gold would be manifest.

As in humans, the adipose of middle-age moderates the capers of youth, so by the time the site of Cymer abbey, the 12th century Cistercian foundation of Llywelyn ap Iorwerth dedicated to the Blessed Virgin, is reached, the river has sobered into a solemnity appropriate to its nuptials with the Wnion. Actually the wedding simile is apt, since until recent times the river's name changed at the confluence to plain "Maw" – hence Barmouth in Welsh remains Abermaw rather than Abermawddach.

The abbey, an offshoot of Abbey Cwmhir in mid Wales, was near the site of the ancient fortress of Cymer which Uchtryd ab Edwin, Lord of Meirionnydd erected in defiance of his Powys overlords Einon ap Cadwgan and Gruffudd ap Maredudd. Reacting immediately, they [a]: destroyed it, [b]: ran Uchtryd out of town and [c]: incorporated Meirionnydd into Powys.

The Abbey was supported by various Welsh princes such as Maredudd ap Cynan and his brother Gruffudd and in 1209 Llywelyn Fawr (*'the Great'*) gifted *"-the rights for digging out and carrying away metals and treasures in mountains and groves."*

It also owned a forge, bred fine horses for the nobility and *"was in possession of many a grassy vale where little but the lowing of their herds and the bleating of their flocks broke the august silence of the mountains."*

Despite this, a lack of arable land, limited fishing rights and a refusal to be involved in the sale of Indulgences, meant that Cymer never became a wealthy foundation. Added to this, with most of their land at high levels, they were particularly affected by the chillier climate that set in during the early 14th century and in fact the monks were never able to afford to complete the building of the Abbey Church.

Thus when Thomas Cromwell, Henry VIII's hit man, showed up with his heavy mob in 1536, he found precious little to pillage, especially as Cymer's one great treasure, its prized chalice and paten, were hidden and remained so for 400 years. However, the "slighted" buildings did provide a source of materials for the good

people of Llanelltyd.

Curiously, although the silverware never reached King Henry, it did fall into the hands of his distant successor George V. It was found by 2 prospectors in 1890 but was never declared Treasure Trove and although the finders got nothing, it changed hands for increasing sums until, in 1910, it was bequeathed to the then new King who lodged it with the National Museum of Wales.

The "Big House" hereabouts was Hengwrt, which was occupied by an offshoot of the Vaughans of Nannau, their most famous scion being Robert Vaughan the great 17th century antiquarian, grandson of Lewis Owen, who had been lynched at Llidiart y Barwn by the bandits of Dinas Mawddwy.

Such families and estates began to appear at the end of the 14th century when the depopulation and social upheavals following the Black Death. *"The ruthless plague that hath neither mercy nor fair countenance"*, helped put an end to *Gavelkind* whereby, on a landowner's death, his holdings were divided between all offspring. This ancient Welsh system of inheritance was replaced by the English *Primogeniture*, the "eldest cops the lot" system that, combined with judicious marriages, concentrated land holdings.

The "Free" village of Llanelltyd, set at the last chance to ford the river unaugmented by the waters of the Wnion, much predates the creation of Dolgellau. Here a church was founded in the 7th century by St. Illtyd himself who, like a number of his protégé saints, embarked at Porthmawr near St. Davids and sailed north, founding churches in the valleys around Bae Ceredigion. Part of Illtyd's mission to the whole Celtic world was to reverse the lapse back into druidism that had followed the end of Roman rule. The mutation from Illtyd to Elltyd reflects the Brithionic influence in the north as opposed to the Geidelic derivations of the south, and is

an early manifestation of the north/south linguistic distinctions that survive in Wales to this day.

It has been said that the six centuries between the departure of the Romans and the Norman Conquest formed the most important era in the development of what we now call Wales. Being largely untroubled by the Vikings and unsullied by Angle, Saxon or Jute, Wales could develop uninterrupted by foreign incursions. Admittedly bullyboys from Ireland caused bother from time to time, but they were fellow Celts who imposed no alien cultures.

The present church at Llanelltyd contains the enigmatic *Kenyric* "footprint" stone and stands in a circular churchyard that formed a sanctuary where a miscreant could remain immune from the law for seven years and seven days. Legend has it that the area of such a "Llan" was defined by a ploughman standing on the proposed site of the altar and with arms outstretched, sweeping his team of eight oxen in a circle.

It was at Llanelltyd at this intersection of trade routes that God met mammon. On the one hand the contemplative tranquillity of Cymer Abbey and on the other the bustle of commerce at this confluence of rivers and roads, and from around 1790 the mining of metals which the good Brothers of Cymer had never fully exploited. This dichotomy is typified by *"Yr Hen Dafarn"* a house tight against the churchyard wall that was once a pub, a rowdy resort of gold miners. Allegedly the additional door on the south of the church was to facilitate access to the inn by thirsty choristers. As a further paradox this inn was the headquarters of the local temperance movement.

This village at the upper limit of Mawddach navigation became the window on the world for Dolgellau and its hinterland, from where ships took costly bales of wool downriver to be carried across the oceans.

The 15th century bridge which reinforced Llanelltyd's trade route importance still stands, although now carrying nothing heavier than a tandem bicycle.

Here "Storehouse" as a modern name is a vestige of the warehouses that held the imports and exports carried on the ships built by the shipwrights at adjoining Maes y

Garnedd. It was said that the soil and the microclimate of the valley flanks produced less durable oak than say the Dyfi or further north, the Dwyryd, but this may have been a slander, whispered by the rival builders. Right or wrong, in the 19th century, Master Shipwrights, Griffith Davies, and Griffith Owen built some 30 fine ships in the yards of those entrepreneurs Robert Jones and Robert Roberts *(Bob y florin)*. On the Mawddach as a whole, up to ten ships per year were completed, making it the third largest Welsh shipbuilding centre after Porthmadog and Pwllheli. Most were Sloops, Brigs or Snows, with some schooners and even full rigged ships.

(Sloops were single-masted, schooners multi-masted, with fore and aft rigs; Brigs were two-masted and Ships three-masted, square-rigged. Snows were Brigs with a small auxiliary after-mast, carrying a spanker-sail.)

Launchings, which were invariably made by women, were usually accompanied by a religious service and sermon and often by an especially composed poem. Usually the dead hulls were towed by rowing boat to Barmouth to be rigged and fitted out.

It was this shipbuilding tradition that helped to ensure the supremacy of the wood-worker in the pecking order of trades. The Welsh name for a carpenter, *saer,* implies skill and the suffixed versions *saer maen* or *saer cerrigs* for a mason imply a lesser skill. An architect is dismissed in Welsh as a mere *pensaer* or head carpenter.

Although so many vessels were built, each taking a year or more to complete, there were periods when yards were idle. It was then that these highly skilled shipwright/carpenters found land-based employment on house building, as up to fairly recent centuries timber or at least timber-framing has been the material of choice for the abodes of the gentry, brick being the sign of an "arriviste" and stone being unacceptably

downmarket.

As far as shipbuilding was concerned, the sessile oak growing into contorted shapes on the steep valley sides formed the frames, closely spaced in the Welsh fashion, with the planking coming from the tall straight pines of North America. Unfortunately, by the 1880s Canada and Newfoundland were able to supply a complete vessel, fitted and rigged, for little more than the cost of the cladding timber. From then on it took a faith in Welsh ships that bordered on bigotry to order a locally-built vessel. In any case by then the superiority of the steel hull was established and ship sizes were outgrowing the capacity of local ports.

Downstream of Llanelltyd the character of the river changes, its two flanks, besides sharply parting company, become diverse. The north bank steep and rugged as if defending itself from its rape by gold diggers, copper miners, manganese merchants and those seeking its hard-as-iron slate. It was here that industry originated when in 1209 Llywelyn granted the monks of Cymer the rights to dig for metals.

The south bank remained gentler, more agrarian, its marshes and wildlife in the guardianship of landowners and estates, seemingly resisting the onslaught of exploitation.

Llanelltyd itself is now a dormitory for Dolgellau. Barely impeded by a speed limit and a roundabout, traffic rushes non-stop over the new bridge with scarcely an eye for the village.

MAWDDACH
4
DOLGELLAU

Dolgellau, the county town of Meirionnydd, is glowered over by Cadair Idris, the chair where the giant Idris rested from his seven-league strides across the Irish Sea. It was an 11th century serf village created by Owain ap Cadwgan ap Bleddyn ap Cynfan, Prince of Powys, Lord of Nannau, nucleated around the well *Ffynnon Mair*. Its prosperity was ensured when Owain's descendant Ynyr Fechan, whose son Meurig is memorialised in Dolgellau church, had the good sense to cooperate with the new regime of Edward I.

It was at Nannau, the ancient settlement awesomely elevated above Dolgellau that Meurig's kinsman, Hywel Sele, had the famous tiff with Owain Glyndŵr. Reputedly this was over hunting rights, but probably arose from Hywel's lukewarm support for Owain's cause. Whatever the reason, Howel vanished and some four decades later a skeleton accompanied by Howel's accoutrements was found in a hollow tree, near where the kitchen garden would later be sited. When the tree fell in 1843 its wood was used to make table-vessels.

In 1880 a vessel of another kind was found at Nannau by General Vaughan - a copper bucket that he used as a receptacle for his cigar ash. In 1951 this ill-considered bucket was recognised as a pricelessly important Bronze Age artefact.

Dolgellau is now a town redolent of the wealth of its wool-driven past, with a market created in the 14th century in defiance of the Royal Prerogative, where the slap of palms determines the destiny of a heifer or a pen of sheep and where the brandishing of walking sticks accompanies every conversation. The town was described by John Ogilvy writing in 1670 as *"An indifferent good market on Tuesday for provisions"*. At about the same time Dolgellau itself was described as – *Tre Gomora myglwyd* ('a smoky Gomorra of a town') not a comment on it's morals but a reflection of the choking fumes of a thousand turf fires that hung over the town.

The 18th century church is in many ways unexceptional, but it was enough to inspire a young worshipper, Edward Bell, to embrace ecclesiastical architecture and to go on to design the Cathedral of St John the Divine in New York.

The glowering granite canyon-like streets squeeze their way around buildings so randomly sited as to almost make negotiation of them call for Ariadne's Minoan thread. Whoever applied the appellation "square" to Eldon, Finsbury, Skinner's and Queen was clearly seriously geometrically challenged.

The buildings are fortress-like, each as solid as a bank, giving the town the confident aura of a mediaeval city-state. The erstwhile gasworks seems a temple homaging some forgotten god of light and the main concourse, Eldon Square, resembles a Greek agora without the sunshine. The likeness of the courthouse (the old County Hall) to a gaol seems to prejudge the guilt of miscreants, although the fact that the original courthouse is now a restaurant suggests a certain refusal to be overawed by the law.

Long before its streets were car-clogged, Dolgellau was a busy town with tanneries, curriers and skinners and, powered by the river Aran, fulling mills and eight factories whose looms filled warehouses with woollen webs for dispatch to America as clothing for slaves.

The web trade (web is actually just a unit of length: 180-200 yards of $31\frac{1}{2}$" wide white cloth) declined after the Napoleonic wars and was abruptly ended by Lincoln's emancipation, and was only partly replaced by flannel making. That was in Victorian times but despite relative isolation, trade and industry had been long developed. Wool weaving began in 1331 when Edward III imported Flemish weavers to set up an industry in the Severn valley. In 1565 this was dignified by a Royal Charter as the Shrewsbury Drapers Company, a concession that a century later Elizabeth I converted into a monopoly, forcing the Welsh weavers and knitters

to sell to the company at whatever price it deigned to offer.

In contrast with most of Wales, Dolgellau took a staunchly Parliamentarian stance during the Civil War. The King's Cavaliers made incursions, but Squire Edward Vaughan, a Roundhead to his bootstraps, saw to it that the Militia made short work of them. Possibly it was this drubbing that caused a Royalist officer to write to King Charles – *"If your highness shall be pleased to command me to the Turk or Jew or Gentils, I will go in my bare feet to serve you but from the Welsh, good Lord deliver us."*

It was this same Edward Vaughan who in 1638 had caused the bridge to be built over the Wnion to meet the needs of the carts and carriages that were beginning to be seen as populations and prosperity recovered from the depredations of the plague of more than two centuries before. He built well; this bridge, twice modified to accommodate by turns a railway and a bypass, can still serve modern traffic.

Despite the town's detestation of Charles I, when "King Billy" displaced James II in 1688, Dolgellau folk joined the Meirionnydd pro-Jacobite riotings.

Yet little more than a decade later Queen Anne saw fit to appoint Edward's grandson Col. Huw Nannau, Vice Admiral for North Wales. Huw remained Welsh-speaking, and employed Siôn Dafydd Las the last household bard in Wales.

A century on the Vaughan name had been re-adopted, and although by this time almost all large landowners were anglicised, Williams Vaughan the great supporter of the revived Eisteddfod and the builder of the present Nannau mansion and much of Llanfachreth as well, stayed loyal to his ancestral tongue. However, in yet a further Vicar of Bray-like veer in loyalties his son, Sir Robert Williams Vaughan, was a rabid Hanoverian royalist. His admiration of George III bordered on the idolatrous, erecting memorials, one English, one Welsh in Llanfachreth churchyard.

AD 1820 To the Memory of George III, King of Great Britain and Ireland. This Structure (together with that of the South Side) intended to preserve the religion which he loved and practiced and to preserve which in its purity was the constant object of his endeavours, through a reign of unexampled length, was erected in the same year which deprived his people of their Father and Friend, by his dutiful and faithfully attached subject, Robert Williams Vaughan.

Llanfachreth was a "one industry village" catering for the needs of Nannau. Its intended location had been Coed Cwm yr Eglwys, the site of Saint Fachreth's cell, but apparently the Devil had other ideas and enforced the present alternative site. The saint himself also had had problems of diabolical origin and had to move into a cave high up the Rhobell Mountain near a holy spring. Later Saint Gwynnog created a holy well and accompanying chapel near Llanfachreth as gesture of sympathy for its having been displaced. It is interesting that although most of the early foundations within reach of the coast such as neighbouring Llanelltyd were initiated by south Wales saints, Fachreth and Gwynnog were north Walians.

By the 18th century Anglicisation was displacing old customs, beliefs and the Bardic tradition. It was scornfully said of the latter *"Wasterly minstrels and other vagabonds, peripatetic poets and musicians are vagrants, legally whippable, stockable and deprivable of their ears."* Actually Methodism played its part as harpist Edward Jones wrote in 1802,

The sudden decline of the national Minstrelsy, and Customs of Wales, is in a great degree to be attributed to the fanatick impostors, or illiterate plebeian preachers, who have too often been suffered to over-run the country, misleading the greater part of the common people from their lawful Church; and dissuading them from their innocent amusements, such as Singing, Dancing, and other rural Sports, and Games, which heretofore they had been accustomed to delight in, from the earliest time. In the course of my excursions through the Principality, I have met with several Harpers and Songsters, who actually had been prevailed upon by those erratic strollers to relinquish their profession, from the idea that it was sinful. The consequence is, Wales, which was formerly one of the merriest and happiest countries in the World, is now become one of the dullest.

Since he did not speak Welsh, Wesley made little impact in Meirionnydd, leaving Calvinism, with its alleged narrowness, free rein and there were those that argued that it was high time, as Dafydd Thomas described Meirionnydd in a poem *Hanes Tair Sir* in1750.

> *Athletic, lusty lively people*
> *Excelling as brave men*
> *Some people here are noted for religion –*
> *But they are only a few.*

Irrespective of cultural erosions, the town was for centuries the distribution centre for the whole of Meirionnydd, with flour, tea, sugar and coal trans-shipped at Barmouth and brought up river to Llanelltyd.

Trade diversified in the late 17th century when John Kelsall opened his blast furnace at Dolgun, where the Clywedog meets the Wnion, which was then navigable to that point. Kelsall may have sited it to be near the ironstone of Bryn Castell, but more likely to be near timber for the charcoal on which his furnace's voracious appetite for fuel depended. It was only in blast for a total of 37 weeks, in that time producing 500 tons of iron. Later it became a forge.

The flourishing woollen manufacture was not confined to factories, every woman knitted. Women carrying baskets of eggs on their heads knitted, farm girls astride bare backed horses dragging sledges knitted, wives and daughters sharing the fireside with the family pig, knitted. Women would gather in each other's houses for communal "knit-ins", like 18th century Tupperware parties; it is said that even whilst engaged in the most intimate activities, women would continue to knit.

Not that there was much profit in it, it was estimated that a woman using wool gleaned from the hedges could only make 1/- (25p) per week knitting stockings full time, which even in 21st century terms would be under £4.00. Less probably than their men folk would spend in the pub while waiting for the wives to finish knitting and get the supper!

What a child made gathering lichens was even more derisory, it would be a good week if a pound weight was harvested, this would fetch 1½ d (0.4p) which would scarcely buy half of a quarten loaf of bread.

By the mid 18th century the Shrewsbury woollen monopoly had become unenforceable and wool was being sent to Prussia, Russia and even more so to the colonies. Trade with Americas was so vital that the War of Independence almost caused panic in the streets of Dolgellau, but once Washington had routed the redcoats of George III, commerce surged. By the end of the 18th century the population had more than doubled to almost 3000.

The town is more welcoming now than in 1781 when Pennant having descended *"By very stony roads"* found *"Every entrance is barred by turnpikes"* and failed to find room at the solitary inn.

A little later the Rev. Bingley had observed the *"place rendered very populous by the very considerable number of manufactories"* and the houses *"Generally low and ill built"* He also remarked on the number of alehouses, quoting Fuller as having written of *"tenements being divided into two or more tippling-houses and chimneyless barns used for that purpose"*. He described his bed at the Golden Lion as *"intolerable"*, but praised the provisions but not the wine upon which, as a late 18th century divine, he was doubtless an expert.

In 1828 *The Post Chaise Companion* was able to name but three houses that took guests, but warned that two of them were not to be recommended as they *"cater for persons without carriages."* Some years later Thackeray said, *"Don't stay at the Lion- there's nothing to put in your belly and the waiters don't answer the bell."* As late as 1885 guide books said that the town was *"in want of a good inn."*

By the end of the 18th century the best days of the Meirionnydd wool trade were over and Dolgellau never fully recovered from the effects of the Napoleonic wars. Although the town did not entirely share the hardships of the more rural parts, in Meirionnydd generally the cost of poor law relief climbed sevenfold between 1776 and 1785, rising a staggering twenty-sevenfold by 1803.

In addition to the deprivation of bread, folk were also deprived of "circuses", with the cessation of that most popular of spectacles, a public hanging; the last taking place in 1813. The star as it were of this final performance was one known as John Greenwell, neé John Ramsbotham, of Lancashire. At this time so many local banks were issuing their own notes that traders had difficulty in keeping track. Forgers tended to use fictitious names under the misapprehension that it was a lesser crime than imitating a genuine bank's specie. Thus when this fellow paid for lodgings and services with Bank of England £5 notes, (which incidentally remained in circulation almost unchanged until the mid 20th century) they were unquestioningly accepted at Aberystwyth, Aberdyfi, Tywyn, Barmouth and so on, as he made his perfidious way up the coast.

However at Dolgellau the landlord of the Golden Lion became very suspicious of a Bank of England fiver he had just been given and consulted Richard Price of Rhiwlas, the biggest landowner in the county and its sheriff, who happened to be lunching at that inn. Price immediately pronounced the note false and learning that the man had ridden north, set off in the hottest of hot pursuits.

On the way he met W.G.Oakeley of Plas Tan y Bwlch who, realising that he had passed the man somewhere near Bronaber, immediately turned his horse to join Price in an impromptu posse. This pair of

lawmen galloping furiously in a manner that would become familiar to cinema-goers a century or so later, eventually cornered the suspect in the stables of an inn at Trawsfynydd.

His pockets having yielded a large quantity of notes only one of which was in any way doubtful, Price was minded to let him go but Oakeley insisted that the varlet be stripped of his breeches. Greenwood's protests at the indignity proved not to be entirely due to modesty or fear of a thrashing, since 39 dud fivers fluttered to the floor.

Roped and bound, Greenwood was frog-marched to Dolgellau. The new gaol not being quite complete, he was incarcerated in the old one (alongside the Aran) but because of its parlous state John Humphreys the blacksmith was directed to fetter him.

At the Assize Greenwood received the mandatory death sentence. Although it was commonplace for persons of influence to seek pardons on behalf of harshly sentenced miscreants, tampering with the currency was felt to threaten the stability of the state and anyway memories of the anti-government riots of the 1790s were still too fresh for any commutation to be sought. Similarly no popular demonstration occurred against the sentence since, although the bilking of innkeepers was considered fair game, it had emerged that Greenwood had also bought a horse with dud notes, which of course placed him beyond the pale, particularly at a time when the war had created a scarcity of good steeds.

In 1814 the old gaol became a madhouse, with the door (the one ended up at Gwynfynydd mine) reinforced by a bolt again made by John Humphreys, who as the gaoler's official blacksmith undoubtedly found crime to be a "nice little earner".

Dolgellau was dramatically and irrevocably changed on 4th August 1868 when the Great Western Railway, under cover of proxy companies, stealthily pushed down from Ruabon in an endeavour to beat the Cambrian Railways to the coast. But the Cambrian swerved inland to thwart the English interloper, eventually meeting it head on at Dolgellau where the two remained like steam stags, antlers locked, each defending its own territory. The station, now crushed to hard-core to build the by-pass, was to the casual eye one complex, but in fact it was in two halves with the CR and the GWR divided by an invisible iron curtain, either side a no-go area for the minions of the opposition. Long after the 1922 shotgun marriage between the two companies, many facilities remained duplicated and for years were respectively identified as "Cambrian" or "GW".

The railways arrived just in time to part-counteract the fallout from the American Civil War, but despite the prosperity it brought and the employment that duplicated station staff demanded, it would never entirely fill the gap left by the loss of the web trade, leaving Dolgellau to be possibly the only town in Britain to be worse off after rail connection. Steam mills failed to halt the decline, but fortunately there was some amelioration in 1888 when it supplanted Harlech as the county town.

By the end of the century, employment was very mixed; the new county functionaries lived among gold miners and slate workers, shopkeepers and coachmen, with blacksmiths well represented. The 1901 census shows 14 of the latter in the town, including at 33 Green Lane next to the Golden Lion Royal, 3 bachelor brothers, an employee, a boarder and a visitor, all six being blacksmith/farriers, this whole Anvil Chorus being looked after by a spinster sister.

Today light industry replaces the woollen sales that did not finally die out until the mid 20th century, but the town is now more bureaucratic than practical, overlooked by the Council Offices rather than by Nannau House. A century or so ago about 10% of the work force were classed as Professional and Administrative, now that figure is almost 50%.

Alongside commerce and industry Dolgellau did not neglect education; John Ellis' Grammar School enrolled its first pupils in 1665, and what is now the Meirionnydd College used to be Dr. Daniel Williams' School for girls. It was established in 1878 by industrialists such as slate magnate Samuel Holland and railway builder Henry Robertson, under the charitable trust set up the eponymous 17th century Wrexham-born Presbyterian divine. It was the Roedean of Wales, but sadly it surrendered to economic pressures in 1975.

Now, thanks to the bypass, it takes two minutes rather than the two hours it previously could take to traverse

the town. However Dolgelllau is not a place to be traversed, rather a place in which to tarry and to savour its solidity, a bastion at the boundary between the mountain and the maritime. Sadly it is no longer possible to buy a gold-miner's pan, W.H.Roberts, more a frontier trading-post than an ironmonger, having succumbed to the economic realities of the third millennium.

Today it is neither wool nor gold that enfames Dolgellau, but Sesiwn Fawr when the town, not to unalloyed approval, is given over to music and poetry and visitors leave their cars on Marian Field where the drovers parked their cattle.

MAWDDACH
5
PENMAENPOOL

Here in 1879 the two banks of the river were tenuously linked by the wooden Pont Borthwnog bridge where the passage of every vehicle sounds like a calamity at a cooperage. This bridge replaced the 16th century ferry for which people waited at what is now the George III Hotel, renamed in deference to Sir Robert Williams Vaughan's Georgomania. Sadly in 1966 the uncertain eddies overturned a pleasure boat against one of its piers, drowning 15 people.

It was here that the ores and the slates from high on Diffwys and the slate dug from the dank chambers at Penrhyngwyn on Cadair were shipped, and the ironstone of Tir Stint began its trip to Brymbo iron works.

On the north bank handy for river transport was an iron forge, the name of the stream that powered it being Mynach (Monk) suggests connection with Cymer Abbey.

Nearby are the Taicynhaeaf (Autumn or harvest houses) a name that may derive from refuges for hill dwellers from the rigours of mediaeval winters, an early example of biannual transmigration.

The higher reaches of the valley have the dreaded pine, but lower down sessile oak maintain their multi-millennia reign.

Penmaenpool, though a smaller shipbuilding centre than Llanelltyd, had deeper water enabling it to construct larger vessels, it being here that Edward Jones, Idris Evans, and timber magnate Watcyn Anwyl launched two-masted Schooners and Brigantines.

One can imagine the stir when one of the perennial rumours of a new order proved correct and that men were actually being taken on, sub-contracts let and timber and fittings ordered. Carpenters, shipwrights and tradesman of every kind, together no doubt with a fair sprinkling of optimistic chancers, would appear as if from nowhere.

Even blacksmiths, although no longer enjoying the mystical status of Celtic times, made enough from shoeings at 2/3d (11p) a round to stand aloof from vulgar solicitation, yet joined the scramble for business.

Brisk trade would be done at the pub as almost every sort of work-seeking trader and tradesman jostled with householders deploring the impending impossibility of having repairs carried out and farmers despairing of finding field labour. At the same time in the same pub, regulars whose maritime experience was limited to being ferried across the river would sagely criticise the choice of rig, pronounce on fine points of hull design and speculate on the choice of Master.

There was, and still is, agriculture on the hill flanks and the river meadows but the "Agrarian Revolution" of Townsend and Coke was slow to arrive and it was near the end of 18th century before improved implements such as the Rotherham plough were widely adopted.

There was some reclamation work done here in the 1870s giving a little extra land but much marsh remained. Thatching reed could be grown, although the usual thatch was made from straw grown on blue or grey lias, with furze as an alternative; reed was the material of choice for the more discerning householder. The 18th century thatchers were, along with the carpenters and blacksmiths, very much top of the tree, capable of making up to 2/- (10p) per day, several times a top ploughman's wages.

Apart from the actual laying, the thatcher would know where to find the best material and just how long to soak it before use to create a part-fermentation which generated the vegetable gluten that made the thatch waterproof.

Slate was dearer to install but cheaper in the long run than thatch, but builders then as now, tended to ignore the long-run economics, particularly with build-to-let property, as thatch maintenance was usually the tenant's responsibility.

40

Thatch became a no-no here in 1865 when the Cambrian Railways arrived. A single glowing speck of soot could destroy in an hour a house lived in for generations. It would be no comfort that the culprit was a magnificent, Oswestry-built, "Large Bogie" 4-4-0 fuelled with the very best that the steam-coal seams of the Rhondda could supply.

Actually both the Cambrian and the Great Western Railways laid claim to this south bank, the Cambrian pre-emptively struck inland to Penmaenpool while the GWR's prodigy, the Bala and Dolgelley Railway, had yet to reach Dolgellau. This was parking their tanks on Paddington's lawn, wars have been fought for less.

Penmaenpool remained the Cambrian terminus until 1868, when they pushed through to Dolgellau. The GWR, its coastal ambitions utterly thwarted, huffed and puffed but after some face-saving mutual running-powers agreements, allowed an end-on junction to be made.

What a sensation the train must have produced, this huge mass of smoke and steel, moving with the power of a hundred horses, uttering the shriek of a maddened banshee! Livestock stampeded, children howled, even the strongest of men quailed, as it approached at unheard of speed, the ground trembling as if facing the wrath of God.

Just short of a century it all lasted, descending from cutting-edge technology, almost to quaint anachronism.

Today the railway's bridges and embankments constructed when engineers ruled the roost and cost accountants knew their place, are silent. The scantily clad successors of the tweed-breeched wheelers and long-skirted, elegantly-hatted lady velocepedistes, who respectfully awaited the monster's passage at level crossings, have now usurped its route, savouring its tranquillity and the variety of its flora.

Abandoned rail track beds tend to be nature rich, providing an environment often tree-screened, free from

traffic disturbance, with features such as cuttings providing microclimates. They often support locally alien plant species, whose seeds were carried from afar by truck and train. Small beasts such as hedgehogs can flourish safe from gypsies, gamekeepers and articulated lorries. Birds can rear their nestlings free from noise and noxious emissions.

At Penmaenpool the car celebrates its victory over the train by parking where the locomotives were shedded. In the signal box that once ruled the route, where only those on the most vital of company business or enjoying the closest acquaintance with the signalman would dare set foot; binocular brandishing bird watchers jostle, since it is now the centre of a prime RSPB bird site. Species such as pied flycatcher and redstart as well as raven and buzzard abound here, at Bont-ddu and at other RSPB sites down river at Arthog as well as the reserve to the east of Dolgellau.

Other railway buildings including the stationmaster's house have been subsumed into the George III Hotel, itself an amalgamation of a 17th century inn and a ships' chandlery warehouse.

This hotel, a focus for bird-watching, walking, fishing and canoeing was blamed, most unjustly of course, for the disappearance of one of a pair of river geese. George the survivor found another mate but when this also vanished the luckless goose sought companionship with a less edible mate – a mooring buoy!

MAWDDACH
6
BONT-DDU

Prior to the "Gold Rush" this place was merely a hamlet where the road from Llanelltyd turned inland, leaving the riverbank that beyond this point was virtually inaccessible except by water. Here Harlech-bound coach travellers fortified themselves for the rigours of the climb over the lonely 2000' Llawlech ridge to Pont Scethin, that solitary bridge where a confluence of tracks and roads formed a veritable Meirionnydd Spaghetti Junction. Indeed rigours they were, there were up-grades where even the inside passengers might be expected to walk, and some where, possibly in freezing rain and cloying mud, they were required to virtually manhandle the vehicle up the rock-strewn track and nearly as terrifying was the ensuing coastward plunge. Incredibly this was almost the only way the then county town of Harlech could be reached from the rest of the Shire. It was also the route, with its still-surviving milestones, whereby drovers from the Ardudwy coast reached the Mawddach; on getting there they presumably felt that the worst part of their journey to London was behind them.

It is on this route a little above the village that in 1832 Robert Williams built a church to save himself the trek to Llanelltyd. The church was completed and duly consecrated, but Williams died before a service was ever held and it stood as a ruin for years, its pews and pulpit ripped apart to provide winter warmth to the upland dwellers. It was restored as a dwelling in the 1870s by John Williams (no relation) the proprietor of the Clogau mine.

Writers found Bont-ddu scarcely worthy of mention; even the garrulous Bingley does not name it, merely referring disdainfully to the piles of drying peat hereabouts.

Then came the gold, a lure for prospectors and speculators as well as hangers-on and harlots. The miners themselves, slaking their gold-induced thirst at the Halfway House, boasted of the strike they would one day make and of the riches that would be theirs. Permeating every corner would have been the thrash of water wheels, the thump of stamps and the grinding of rolls and shaking tables and Britten pans, and of the clank of drams on rails; as high above the village 500 miners in half a dozen and more mines attempted (usually vainly) to induce the recalcitrant rock to yield its treasure. Indeed this village was for half a century and more the focus of a close agglomeration of gold diggings, the very epicentre of the Dolgellau Gold Belt.

As at Cwm Heisian up valley, the miners at St. David's copper mine had realised that they shouldn't be dumping this brassy stuff and metamorphosed their working into Clogau, the most successful of the Welsh gold setts and the only one to survive, albeit on a small scale, into the 21st century. Fabled as a supplier of royal wedding-rings, in 1904 it turned out over half a ton of gold, although it must be said that in most years a tenth of that would be exceptionally good, and a hundredth not unusual.

Not all the mines could afford the luxury of shop-bought tools; stone anvils for the laborious crushing of ores were not unheard of and to some a proper iron hammer as opposed to a handy-sized stone was cutting-edge technology. Even where there was a degree of mechanisation it could be of the most primitive kind; at St. David's mine there are still the traces of an arastra, a device brought from South America by the first Conquistadors consisting of a tapered stone roller dragged around a circular crushing platform. But however primitive their methods, all had the dream that the next barrow-load, or at the very worst the one after, would groan with nuggets.

In fact the entire Welsh output of gold during the late 19th and early 20th centuries totalled around 4

tons, which would make a very valuable lorry-load, but it would not have gone very far supporting up to 600 or more men over several decades. Operations were often dependent on cross subsidy from other metals particularly zinc, demand for which grew with the rise of galvanising in the latter part of the 19th century.

Despite the non-viability of the mines themselves, mining operations were of considerable indirect benefit. Supplies and services were needed, compensating tradesmen and chandlers for the decline in shipbuilding; besides which the mine wage levels drove up earnings generally. In the mining areas of Meirionnydd agricultural wages were typically up to 50% more than in, for instance, the rural areas of Carmarthenshire. Not that this all fed back into the local economy, since comparatively large pay packets created boundless opportunities for entrepreneurs intent on separating men from their money.

Unfortunately the decline of mining coincided with the agricultural hard times of the 20th century and regrettably initiatives such as the Merioneth Mining Development Council of 1930 have failed to create a revival.

Now the tranquil hillside abounds with the ruins of the buildings and the buddles, which with the rail formations and the occasional fragment of rusting machinery, form a jungle habitat for bird and vole, whilst the adits and levels are sanctuaries for bats and the waste heaps host colourful metal-seeking plants and lichens. Walkers who brave the climb to the old goldmine tramway bed, (now dubbed "New Precipice Walk") can enjoy a splendid view, superior to the more publicised Torrent and (Old) Precipice walks at Dolgellau.

In the village it is doubtful if visitors could still purchase a pint for a pinch of gold dust, but on the other hand they are unlikely to be pestered by enterprising urchins intent on selling quartz fragments dazzling with iron pyrites.

Curiously, although the commercial raising of gold in Wales has declined to nominal levels, its retail availability as "Welsh Gold" jewellery seems to continue unabated!

It used to be said that Welsh gold was "darker"; this canard arose because of the custom of alloying it with copper rather than "white" metals such as silver, zinc, tin, cadmium or indium. Actually the origin of gold can only be determined by trace elements detectable solely by delicate testing.

In 1840 as a means of boosting the woollen industry, the Llanelltyd–Barmouth turnpike was built, which when a corresponding road was built beyond Barmouth, the appalling mountain route to Harlech could be abandoned.

This new accessibility enabled the Rev. W. E. Jelf in the 1860's to build Caerdeon Hall in a niche high in the hillside where, overlooking the estuary, he could entertain heavyweight literati such as Ruskin, Tennyson, Wordsworth and Darwin. As a monoglot Englishman he did have a problem, since in Welsh-speaking areas the law demanded that church services be in Welsh. This difficulty was solved by emulating Robert Williams and building his own church which was modelled on a Basque church he had once admired. His brother-in-law, Rev. John Petit who had backed the enterprise moved in with him and conducted the services in English.

The most frightful row ensued, led by the vicar of Barmouth. Protests were long and loud, both the Civil Law and Consistory Courts were invoked but Jelf had the ear of Prime Minister Lord Palmerston who pushed through the English Services in Wales Act 1863, to legalise the Jelf/Petit position.

On Jelf's death in 1875, Samuel Holland bought the Hall retiring there full of years and honours. This was the same

Samuel Holland that aged 23 had walked across Wales to sack and supplant the drunken manager of his father's slate quarry; who in the course of a chance meeting over a pub lunch, founded the Ffestiniog Railway; who built roads, schools and a hospital and helped to turn Blaenau Ffestiniog from a hamlet to a mini-metropolis. Curiously, perhaps tiring of idleness, Holland took out a mining lease on Caerdeon in 1888 although any digging seems to been confined to the horticultural.

A little further along at Glyndŵr, the Afon Dwynant powered a small corn mill; almost inaccessible by land, flour was taken out by boat from the tiny creek where seaweed manure and supplies for the hamlet of Cutiau were landed. It is said that the virtual disappearance of this hamlet was due to the landlord evicting his tenants when, after the turnpike was built blocking the creek, they won the right to load and unload on his land.

Unannounced landing from the river was a constant bone of contention; riverside landowners constantly contested the right of barge crews to cross their land when, due to tidal conditions, they had to temporally beach their vessels. This problem, exacerbated by the bargees penchant for making camp and lighting fires to cook al fresco meals allegedly from purloined produce, only ceased when rail competition ended the barge traffic.

MAWDDACH
7
ARTHOG

Here on the southern side beyond the spook-ridden Abergwynant woods and the other ships' timber nurseries, are the abandoned tips and gaunt structures of the quarries that flourished in the mid-nineteenth century when the world clamoured for Welsh slate.

Although much of their lower area has been removed for bulk-fill, the serried terraces of the Arthog/Ty'n y Coed workings tower crazily above the road where 30 to 40 men toiled on half a dozen levels terraced out of the hillside. A fine embanked formation once carried a tramway across the road and down to a wooden jetty from where barges carried slates across the river to Barmouth, there to be shipped to roof the teeming cotton towns of Lancashire.

There must have been rejoicing when the railway was laid past their front door, no longer would their slates have to be perilously punted across the estuary, individually trans-shipped and shaken and shattered on the stormy seas around the Llŷn peninsular. Now they could be on a roof virtually within hours of being split from the block, a spanking new state-of-the-art mill was built to handle the demand that would surely ensue. With the paradoxical perversity that dogged the Welsh slate industry, the railway also benefited other quarries producing better material, so despite being near the peak of demand, the quarry failed even before rail connection could actually be made. Crazily, when the quarry did re-open with the incline diverted to meet the new Garth siding, it was 1879 the very nadir of the slate trade's fortunes. Working stumbled on for a few brief years before closing right on the eve of the trade recovery. They did have a huge problem of where to put their waste, despite buying the adjoining quarry as a dumping group, their heap (now much removed for hard core) threatened to encroach onto the road.

It is a sad reminder of the true cost of slate that when John Thomas was killed here by a rock fall in 1881, he was but one of half a dozen men who met their deaths in north Wales slate workings that year.

The capacious stockyard is now a caravan site, which is probably its first ever profitable use. The fine stone-built incline still leads down to the ghost of the siding and just a few jutting timbers mark the jetty.

The Mawddach viaduct which ex-draper, sometime coal-owner turned railway contractor/speculator Thomas Savin, defied the laws of nature and of economics to push across the estuary was opened in 1867. Since then it has survived storm, tempest, Dr. Beeching and the Toledo beetle with equanimity.

Exercising understandable caution, locomotives were at first barred from venturing onto it, thus carriages had to be pulled across by horses one at a time. It was only after three months of incident-free operation that complete trains were allowed to go over. One would have thought that trials with locomotives rather than carriages would have provided more effective proof of the bridge's integrity, but then carriages even when full of passengers, were considered more expendable!

At its southern end was Barmouth Junction, a triangular confluence of lines that boasted 5 platform faces, a total that was only matched in Wales by Cardiff General and Swansea High Street. Even those metropolitic stations could not equal its 3 signal boxes. Here passengers on the magnificent Cambrian coastal route which still skirts Bae Ceredigion from Aberystwyth to Pwllheli, could divert inland to Dolgellau and if so wished, continue on the Great Western to Bala and the valley of the Dee.

Until the Great Western's braggadocio overcame their economic sense and they built their Bala-Blaenau branch in the 1880s, this route was the sole (and circuitous) connection between Blaenau Ffestiniog, the burgeoning commercial powerhouse of Meirionnydd and Bala, its emotional epicentre.

Besides acting as a junction, the triangle could also served to turn locomotives, a valuable function since land constraints virtually proscribed a turntable at Barmouth. With the inland connection gone, the sad remnant of this complex is now dubbed Morfa Mawddach serving the Arthog Bog Nature Reserve but not much else. Although called a station, it is but a single platform unmanned halt that provides scant shelter from the winds that, except at the pinnacle of summer, are embittered by the Atlantic wastes and pierce the stoutest garment with the ease of a thermic lance.

On the hill nearby is Tyddyn Sieffre, the farm from where Thomas Pugh left to join the Dolgellau Quakers in Pennsylvania in 1695. Slate for export from Barmouth and stone for building the viaduct was quarried here and taken by tramway to the wharf at Feglas Fawr.

In the last years of the 19th century, Cardiff draper Solomon Andrews attempted to outdo McDougall's efforts at Fairbourne by creating a "family" seaside resort in the Feglas area using the tramway to bring down stone from Tyddyn Sieffre quarry and landing other building material at the wharf. Besides houses that "respectable persons" could rent he planned shops, hotels, a park and public buildings, but only got as far as part-building his Mawddach Crescent and his St.Mary's and Glaslyn Terraces, the sole public edifice being a tin shed "refreshment rooms".

These oddly out-of-place suburban-style houses were served by two horse-drawn cars on the Tyddyn Sieffre industrial tramway which was re-laid and extended to run from the main road and the railway to the viaduct where the lower deck of a Cardiff horse-tramcar, displaced by electrification, did duty as a waiting room.

This attempt to create Llandudno-on-the-Mawddach was a failure partly due to lack of takers and partly (like Savin at Ynys-las 30 years before) due to subsidence. One of the trams was transferred to the Pwllheli-Llanbedrog tramway where Andrews' ambitions found more success. The other continued to ply here until 1905 when having also failed to establish himself at Aberdyfi, Andrews admitted defeat and withdrew to the security of his south Wales emporia.

Isolated and with all the drawbacks of coastal living with few of the advantages, it proved difficult to find occupiers for even the few houses that were completed. They were eventually let on peppercorn rents creating a role for the settlement as an artists' colony.

It briefly saw feverish activity during WW2 as a Royal Marines training base prior to the D-day Normandy landings before resuming its unfashionable obscurity.

MAWDDACH
8
FRIOG & FAIRBOURNE

Right on the cusp of coast where the estuary becomes the sea is Fairbourne, a place that does not seem to be able to make up its mind what it wants to be; working village, dormitory settlement or holiday resort.

At one time there were just a few farmers and fishermen to be found here at what was then still known as Ynys Faig; plus occasionally a few hardy souls committing themselves to the perils of the ferry from Penrhyn Point to Barmouth.

The ferry was established in 1569, barely a year into the reign of Elizabeth I and it has survived the railway competition by offering transit cheaper than the train and less taxing than the walk across the viaduct.

Like most places along the coast there have been many tales of smuggling, one at least being somewhat bizarre. It appears that in 1780 a David Williams of Henddol bought some goods from a Frenchman but omitted to pay for them, apparently judging that since the goods were smuggled the debt would not be pursued. In the event the Frenchman did seek enforcement from the Deputy Sheriff Owen Owens. When Owens sent a posse to confront Williams and his cronies, an "OK Corral" style shoot-out ensued with Owens and two of his bailiffs being hurt and having to be ferried to Barmouth for treatment. It seems that Williams escaped unscathed and since the lawmen did not relish a rematch, Williams remained unapprehended, leaving the Frenchman to ponder on the ways of the Welsh.

The area came to prominence in 1793 when no fewer than five persons from the area, four of them women, one of whom was suckling a child, stood in the dock at the "Spring Great Sessions" at Bala charged with the capital offence of sheep stealing. Piquancy was added by the fact that three of the female defendants were a mother Catherine and her two daughters Sarah and Mary. Sarah had a *"base child"* and Mary had previously been imprisoned and publicly flogged at Dolgellau for stealing *a pair of sheets valued at ten pence* (4p). The trio apparently maintained a ménage at Brynhir where men were made more than welcome.

The clientele of such an establishment would presumably have been drawn from the lower orders, as the uchelwyr (upper class) in need of compliant female company would have recourse to maidservants or the daughters of tenants. However, since coins of the Realm were strangers to lesser men's pockets, the ladies had to accept settlement of their professional fees in chattels, which regrettably were often stolen.

Finding various sundry items missing, a local innkeeper Meredith Howell laid information against them, a warrant was issued and their home searched by two *"Petty Constables"*. Various items of property belonging to Howell and others was found, but more seriously, so were the *"Mortal components"* of four sheep and corresponding fleeces carrying the earmark of neighbouring farmer John Rees.

Being Saturday, the two constables, Howell and John Rees kept the women under house arrest pending matters being be dealt with on the Monday morning. It appears that the mother and daughter Sarah entertained their captors so cordially that when Monday came Mary was found to have escaped!

Mary was eventually recaptured at Pennal and the three were jointly charged with the theft of *"4 coarse napkins valued at one shilling (5p), 3 fat geese valued at three shillings, a brewing sieve valued at half a crown (12.5p) and a sack valued at three shillings."* Plus with stealing *"4 sheep valued at one pound"*.

Mary stated that one William German, a Pembrokeshire miner, then employed in Ceredigion, had stolen and slaughtered the sheep. Presumably he was "passing trade" paying for services rendered that, since he allegedly was also responsible for the theft of the geese, the sieve and the sack, must have been exceptionally satisfactory. She also implicated a mysterious man living across the river at Barmouth, described as her

mother's "husband" but apparently not the father of either girl. Oddly no attempt seems to have been made to find, let alone apprehend, either man. These events having taken place in the middle of the previous December, the meat, the poultry and indeed the napery were clearly destined for festive tables. The purpose of the brewing sieve and sack is less obvious unless they played some obscure role in the ladies' activities.

A few days later, Edward John of Eglwys Goed was actually seen in the act of stealing sheep from Pant y Llan and afterwards he and his wife were caught literally "red handed" having just slaughtered an ewe.

For some reason the charges against John's wife were struck out but he and the other women stood trial, and inevitably were sentenced to be *"conveyed to the common place of Execution in this County. And to be then and there each of them respectively hanged by their respective Necks until they be respectively dead"*.

Fortunately for them, their judge was one of a growing number who opposed such severe penalties and he immediately lodged Petitions of Pardon supported by various local notables including Sir Robert Vaughan of Nanney.

This resulted in stays of execution and eventual commutation to seven years transportation in the case of Catherine, Sarah and Edward John. By some legal quirk these sentences were actually served in Britain, not necessarily the preferred option since a transportee's lifestyle was far better than that endured in one of the mediaeval dungeons that passed for county gaols. Mary remained under the shadow of the noose for eight years until she was reprieved to suffer transportation to New South Wales where she died, apparently a widow, in the mid 1830s; probably Merionethshire's first Antipodean emigrant.

Incidentally this failure to immediately carry out death sentences was seriously unpopular with local

burgesses since they had to bear the cost of feeding and guarding the prisoners whilst the lawyers wrangled. For the same economic reason bail was often granted for most serious offences.

Much of Fairbourne was built in the late 1890's by Mr. Arthur (self-raising flour) McDougall seeking to emulate Savin's seaside resort ambitions at Ynys-las and elsewhere. He was more successful than Savin and for that matter, his neighbour Andrews, but the final product fell far short of his original vision of a whole "New Town".

He used bricks from his own on-site brickworks; this works being connected to the site by a horse-drawn tramway. This tramway was extended in 1898 to serve the ferry and a new railway station which was built on the site of the 1865-67 temporary "Barmouth Ferry Station" from where passengers were taken by carriage to Penrhyn Point during the months between the line being opened and the viaduct being completed. Since they correctly forecast that such a station would be uneconomic, the Cambrian Railways demanded a contribution of £500 from McDougall towards its cost.

This new station included a pre-existing siding used by Henddol slate quarry so Mr. McDougall planned to recoup his expenditure of £700, plus the payment to the railway, by imposing a toll on the passage of slates over his land. Since the quarries had been loading onto the railway for some 30 years, this gambit was a trifle cheeky and unsurprisingly the railway vetoed it.

Anticipating modern "English v Welsh" place-name disputes, the residents wanted the station named Ynys Faig, but McDougall wanted Fairbourne, so on the pretext that the sign had already been painted, Fairbourne it was.

The Henddol quarry had been started in 1865 by Dr. Walker, a surgeon from Nottingham, who formed a company managed by local farmer and fellow Quaker Howell Jones Meredith but due to a fall of rock the business was wound up in 1871. Dr. Walker concentrated his attentions on the adjacent Goleuwern quarry, which after a period of idleness in the late 1870s was reunited with Henddol as G. A. Walker & Co., Henddol being energetically worked underground. An incline brought material from the combined working down to road level, but its planned tramway connection to the station was never built. Walker having died in 1884, the whole passed to Mr. Abel Simner in 1892. Trading as Cambrian Estates, Howell was retained as Henddol manager with his son Edward in charge of Goleuwern. They employed some 80 men, loading onto rail around 30 tons of slate per week, but by the end of the century stiff competition from the big Caernarfonshire quarries who were producing the same Cambrian slate of better quality, robbed them of much business. Circa 1898 McDougall bought part of the site, the Goleuwern workings then being in a deep pit accessed by a tunnel. The tunnel was blocked and the Panteinion stream diverted to convert the pit into a reservoir, which was to feed an hydroelectric plant in a building at the foot of the incline. Although never completed it has left one delightful legacy, the "Blue Lake", which like so many other abandoned quarries, has sheer rock faces that encourage nesting by birds such as ravens, chough and even gulls.

Near the entrance to the dry upper tunnel which gives access to the Blue Lake is the unique 5'9" incline-head sheave wheel that Dr. Walker had specially cast by De Winton's of Caernarfon.

Work continued at Henddol with final closure coming in 1928 but Edward's son Howell remained in the district until his death in 1991.

There were other slate quarries whose trifling output scarcely registered on railway, or indeed any other records, These included the remarkable Cyfannedd, on land chartered by Llywelyn Fawr to Cymer abbey in 1209, which circa 1870 converted itself from a lead mine into an underground slate working.

Above the notorious Friog rocks at Ty'r Allt was the most westerly of the Mawddach gold workings. Ore from a small adit was crushed in a mill that squeezed tight alongside the railway line and powered by a 50' waterwheel was fed from a leat off the river Caletwr. It was here that one of the very few loss of life accidents suffered by Cambrian Railways occurred. In 1883 due to a landslide a locomotive was derailed and crashed onto the rocks killing both footplate men, both curiously, named William Davies.

Fairbourne's chief fame now rests on the narrowest of Wales' narrow gauge railways, the $2^1/_2$ mile Fairbourne Railway. Unlike the other "Great Little Trains of Wales" it was not derived from a former freight line, but was laid down as an "attraction", anticipating the perception of a railway as a ride rather than a journey by half a century. It follows the route of McDougall's line re-laid in $12^1/_2$" gauge with models of main line engines as motive power. Far from being just a toy railway it still takes passengers to the Summer-run Barmouth ferry.

MAWDDACH
9
BARMOUTH

Barmouth, or 'Bermo in the economical speech of the area, crowds improbably onto a tiny spit of land with homes and chapels Velcroed to its rock-face backdrop, each looking down the chimneys of their neighbours. It was alleged that the inhabitants in some parts of the town *might almost cure their bacon by hanging it out of their windows*.

Its history much predates chapels and indeed homes, only a little to the north at Morfa Dyffryn low tide reveals petrified tree-stumps and crude deer antler tools. As well as such pre-historic vestiges, Romano/Christian standing stones are reminders both of the Celtic Saints and of the tradition of coastal seafaring that enabled them to reach here from the south.

It was here legend has it that in Tŷ Gwyn, the house of Gruffudd Fychan, the negotiations for the Earl of Richmond, the future Henry VII, to march from Pembroke to Bosworth were conducted. Certainly isolation made it ideal for covert activities, indeed this isolation gave rise to many accounts of smuggling over the years with the usual legends of customs men being unable to obtain convictions for what local juries considered a legitimate activity.

There was even talk of piracy, an Elizabethan survey of 1565 reported –

"Abermowe being likewise a haven for pirates having no habitacion. But only foure howse, whereof there are Owners, Res ap Res, Harry ap Eden, Thomas ap Edward and John ap Hoel Gocheand there is neither shipp nor vessell that belongeth to the same haven. But only towe litle Bootes that the said Res ap Res and Harry a Eden do use to cary men over that passaige, whereof we have deputed Moryce ap Hoel Bedo and Eden ap Hoell ap Gruffith."

Counties had Vice Admirals, not seafaring men but local worthies charged with the suppression of piracy and other maritime naughtinesses, but there is no record of any of those of Meirionnydd having ever been seriously involved in suppressing such activities.

Shortly following the survey, Barmouth benefited from the Elizabethan growth of sea trade so that by the time of Thomas Pennant's late 18th century visit it was a vital port of almost 1500 inhabitants trading with Spain and Italy, although Pennant berated the inhabitants for their lack of enterprise in allowing the woollen trade amounting to £40,000 and the stocking trade of £10,000 per annum to be *"conducted by agents"*.

Despite alleged failures to maximise opportunities, wool brought considerable prosperity, indeed by then some hundred vessels belonged to the port. These took on board animals and butter, timber and wood bark, bagged ores of copper and of lead as well as painstakingly packed slates, besides the webs from Dolgellau and stockings from Bala; all brought down river to be re-loaded into deep-sea vessels. These ships arriving at the rate of three or four per week brought in every sort of necessity to a town that, until the turnpike from Dolgellau was built, was virtually inaccessible by land and to reach it by boat from "The Stoves" (Llanelltyd) cost 3/6 (17.5p) per head, equivalent to perhaps £10 in modern values.

Increasingly as agriculture improved, limestone to be burnt at kilns along the river also became prominent in Barmouth's maritime trade.

Most of these sea-going ships were locally manned and, despite allegations of the inferiority of Mawddach oak, many were Barmouth-built. Between 1780 and 1880 dynasties of Jones, Griffiths, and Evans launched more than 80. This fleet, augmented by ships built up river, not only handled Barmouth trade but also carried Porthmadog and Caernarfon slate to the Americas and beyond. Eventually the locality had its own shipping line, the Aberdyfi & Barmouth Steamship Company of 1892, owned by prosperous grocers of the two towns.

The cramped nature of 19th century Barmouth is illustrated by the account of how, when the schooner "Hirnant" was built, it overhung the main street to such an extent that at its launch the traditional bottle-

breaking was conducted from a bedroom window on the landward side of the street!

Despite the town's inaccessibility and being considered *"Inferior to Tenby as a bathing place"* it found increasing favour with visitors although they were warned of the number of pigs laying about the streets, which *"shared the peasants' turf-warmed cottages by night"*. It would be well into the 19th century before coal appeared in any but the wealthiest of households.

Apparently Barmouth's popularity amongst *"Genteel families"* as a health resort arose from the alleged curative properties of the Scurvy Grass that grew on the banks of the estuary.

The Rev. Bingley found much to criticise. *"This town is situated in one of the most unpleasant places that could have been chosen for it. - the lower parts are rendered dirty by the drifting sand, which fills every passage and is blown into every window"*. In addition he found that the three bathing machines *"Altogether appropriated for the use of ladies"*, gentlemen having to, (shock horror!) *"Bathe on the open coast"*.

Although he found the lodging houses *"dirty and miserable places"*, he was delighted with the Corsygedol Arms, partly due to the civility of Mrs Lewis the innkeeper, but chiefly because most of his fellow guests were persons of *"fortune and fashion"*. (Indeed Barmouth has invariably regarded itself as being slightly upmarket.)

It attracted visitors such as Wordsworth who, on his first visit in 1824 when rowing a hired skiff (presumably urged by sister Dorothy), described the estuary as *"Sublime, which may compare with the finest in Scotland"*.

By 1834 crime in Barmouth called for the erection of a "Round House" containing two cells one for men and one for women. In such lockups, a common feature of Welsh towns, the Parish Constable could, without recourse to judges or magistrates, summarily incarcerate any citizen manifesting signs of obstreperousness – a

system that many feel might well be revived. Although deeply insalubrious, it was better than some "Houses of Correction" and certainly better than the original windowless dungeon at Dolgellau where the inmates were chained to the wall.

The roads had brought prosperity, but the opening of the rail viaduct in 1867 was bad news dealing a terminal blow to the port which was exacerbated by the web trade virtually vanishing after the American Civil War. In 1867 169 vessels had loaded at Barmouth, the next year a mere 89 and by 1871 there were just 11, although groceries and other supplies from Liverpool continued to come in by sea, the *S.S. Telephone* being a weekly visitor around the turn of the century. In fact, right up to the 1930s, shopkeepers' errand boys with trolleys were still meeting boats on the quayside.

Fortunately tourism and well-heeled settlers to some extent filled the void left by the decline of seafaring. These latter formed English congregations that augmented the Welsh-speaking chapels that Victorian

religiosity demanded. Indeed the south Wales based religious revival of 1904 made much impact on the town and the ghostly apparition of the "Man in Black" was taken to be a manifestation of Evan Roberts, the Loughor evangelist.

The prosperity of the town had been boosted in the 1880s by manganese mining. Since the 1820s a little ore had been raised locally to meet a miniscule chemical market but the growth of steel-making created a huge demand. Some half a dozen mines and cuttings were worked in the town's immediate hinterland.

As tonnages grew an aerial ropeway from the mines to Barmouth was planned but with richer and cheaper foreign ores becoming available, the industry declined and had all but vanished by the end of the century. During WW1, due to a combination of strategic necessity and Lloyd George's encouragement of Welsh industry, production was temporarily resumed. In WW2 the need for Welsh ore was, if anything, greater but working was almost entirely confined to the better ores of Penllyn.

The resources on which the town depends are no longer extracted from the ground, but

from the pockets of visitors, the grand "villas" built for wealthy retired folk having become boarding houses. One attraction is Dinas Oelu mansion, the first property to be bought by the National Trust; also extant are Tŷ Gwyn, the Gaol, and the 1890s Sailors Institute and Reading Room.

. Barmouth is a great boating centre, well removed from the "gin & tonic" image of the more fashionable marinas. The highlight of the maritime year is the start of the Three Peaks Race which demands that teams of 5 (3 seamen and 2 runners) sail up the west coast of Britain, pausing successively to land at Caernarfon, Whitehaven and Fort William, covering 389 miles by boat under canvas, 18 miles of cycling, 72 miles of running and a total of 14,000' gain of height.

Almost as strenuous is the 7-mile hill run, but more sedentary are the July Music Festival and the September Arts Festival.

Barmouth's fishing heritage is now magnificently proclaimed by the millennium sculpture on the seafront *"The Last Haul"* created by local sculptor Frank Coxley. It also pays homage to the town's maritime trading past since it was carved from a block of Carrera marble raised from a Genoese ship that was wrecked off Tal-y-bont in 1709. This wreck, or perhaps two merged wrecks, is known as the "Bronze Bell Ship" and was regarded as one of the most important maritime finds ever found on the Welsh coast.

"THE LAND BETWEEN"

Rhwng y Ddwy Afon
(Between the Two Rivers)

CADAIR IDRIS

CADAIR IDRIS

Ranking twelfth in summit height, Cadair is an also-ran by Snowdonia standards but being decidedly visible, readily accessible and with a punchy name, it is the best known and most visited summit in Wales after Snowdon itself. It offers the adventure of a mountain climb without excessive effort; whilst it is a cliché to talk about panoramic views, the ridge does offer more likely prospects than mist-shrouded Snowdon. It is said that to spend a night at its summit risks transformation into a poet or a lunatic – but that is said about almost every peak in Wales.

It is possible although not at all easy, to reach the summit by following Afon Aran, the river that once drove the water wheels of Dolgellau's mills. It was in this Afon Aran that in 1877 a human arm was found, allegedly discovered through its interfering with the wheel of the fulling mill. A diligent search of the river yielded a complete set of body parts which were identified as the remains of missing farm servant Mary Hughes of Brithdir for whom police had been searching for some time.

Fellow farm-worker Cadwaladr Jones was quickly arrested and due to his local popularity was tried and condemned at Chester.

It emerged that Jones, a married man, having made the young woman pregnant, killed and buried her in his garden, but with both the police and his wife becoming suspicious at his newfound interest in horticulture, he disinterred the body, dismembered it and disposed of it in the Aran. He was brought back to Dolgellau to be hanged amid vociferous protests that he should be spared on the grounds that Mary was a "notorious fornicator"; the "two-to-tango" element implicit in her "condition" seems to have been overlooked.

A less unfortunate resident of the hamlet of Brithdir was the Reverend Charles Tooth retired chaplain to the Anglican community of Florence. In 1896 in order to provide a tangible souvenir of his service in sunnier climes and presumably to have somewhere to go on a Sunday, he built himself a church in the Italianate style, somewhat in emulation of the Caerdeon "Basque" church. Although the exterior is unexceptional, the interior pays respect to vernacular materials in a most exceptional fashion. The pulpit and other parts are embellished with beaten copper of extraordinary quality and the equally fine font honours, lead – another product of the locality.

On this eastern flank of Cadair commanding the valley of the Wnion, the Romans built a fort but the area is now less prized for military advantage than for the alliterative roll-call of its bird life - woodlarks and wheat ears, willow tits and winchats.

Ascending this way past where clubmoss and orchid nestle under the sycamores, hollies and oaks takes one near Bryn Mawr, the home of Rowland Elis who emigrated in 1657 to Pennsylvania; one of a strong contingent of Meirionnydd Quakers who sought freedom of worship in that colony. Ellis took his house name with him which eventually became the home of the poshest of posh academies for the daughters of the Daughters of the American Revolution. Although the 17th century emigrations left Meirionnydd almost a Quaker-free zone, they did leave their hats behind – that of the archetypal Puritan man being adopted as women's headgear when Lady Llanover and others re-invented "Welsh Costume" in the 19th century.

However, regardless of tradition or attire, continuing on the metalled road to Bwlch Coch gives a thousand feet of motorised bonus before one plods the precipices above.

On the Tal-y-llyn pass the presence of cicely and of spignel, its most southerly known occurrence, suggests a planting by herbalists long ago.

The shortest ascent is from Minffordd; here is Dolau Cae where, on the site of a 14th century house lived Howell Idris MP, the founder of the "Idris" fizzy drinks empire. From here a stiff climb takes one high over that prince of mountain lakes Llyn Cau. Challenging but more rewarding is the Fox's Path passing the two lakes Gadair and its little sister Gafr. Llyn y Gadair in its chair-like corrie is of course the legendary seat of the giant whose full name was Idris Gawr, although always know as Idris, with a guy that size "Mr. Cawr" would seem to be a wiser form of address.

Actually gadair besides literally meaning "chair" can also mean the "place of", analogous to the English

"country seat", so that the name is likely to have referred to the purview of some ancient chieftain and the legendary size may have referred to his influence and intellect rather than his stature. One can approach from the south west, from Llanfihangel home of Mary Jones who walked barefoot to Bala to find a Welsh Bible but least taxing is the Pony Path. It is indeed rideable and once one could make the trip on hired donkey. Legend apart, the main joy of this route is the vista over the estuary – giving one every excuse for breathtaking pauses, and that reminder of industry, the ruins of Penrhyngwyn slate quarry whose products were pack-horsed down alongside the tumbling cataracts of the aptly named Gwynant ('white stream').

Part of the mountain is designated a National Nature Reserve with a range of grasslands, much bilberry heath and areas of montane moss heath.

There are also mires and on the lower ground, remnants of sessile oak woodland and it is also one of the most southern habitats in Britain for arctic-alpine plants such as least willow and purple saxifrage. It is in heights like this that tendrils of the ancient bardic metempsychosis, the migration of the souls of the dead, lurked in the crevices of Christian belief as an 18th century traveller found one winter's night at a one-roomed cottage not that far way on the Clwydian hills.

An old woman was struggling to free the solitary, long unopened window and as he went to assist her he saw that her husband lay dead on the bed. Besides bereavement at the loss of her lifetime companion, she undoubtedly faced destitution yet her only thought was to ensure that his immortal soul's ascent should be unimpeded.

The Rev. Bingley took the Minford Path although one would be now hard pressed to find Llyn Trigrainwyn, the "Pool of the Three Pebbles" that he made much of. It is now filled in, the road cuts though its

site at the head of the Tal-y-llyn pass. Part of it, which was nearer fifty inches deep rather than its reputed fifty fathoms, now forms a lay-by leaving high and dry the three rocks which the giant Idris allegedly tipped out of his shoe.

Bingley was impressed by Cadair but less so was his fellow cleric, Francis Kilvert who climbed in heavy rain, describing it as *"the stoniest, dreariest, most desolate mountain"*. A few years previously Tennyson had climbed also in rain and had descended in odeless saturation.

Bingley spent two nights at the foot of Y Gadair at the Blue Lion, a small public house that, like most he encountered in Wales, was not to his liking. Referring to the provisions he said, *"The negative catalogue was copious"*. It appears that no meat other than bad bacon was available, nor were there any eggs, wines or spirits. The landlord, Edward Jones he described as *"a schoolmaster, guide and cutter of gravestones, with a considerable taste for ale and somewhat too talkative particularly on the subject of his own qualifications."*

The made-on-the-premises ale reinforced by bread and butter apparently represented Bingley's tea, supper, dinner and breakfast for the next two days. Bingley was charged 2/6d (12.5p) for the food and the bed, and the same sum for the ale. Since this would have purchased 30 pints, his criticism of the landlord's thirst were surely challengeable.

Whilst critical of the comestibles, he did admit that *"the bed was not a very bad one,"* and he was *"not so pestered with fleas as at Beddgelert"* (the predecessor to the present "Goat" at Beddgelert was notorious for the savagery of its parasites) By Bingley's time accommodation was improving, but damp, flea-ridden straw-palliased cots were still commonplace in the country. He did enjoy the luxury of a room to himself; many travellers often had to endure sharing rooms with fellow guests, and even possibly the landlord's children and

servants. The presence of rats was so universal as not to merit mention.

Conditions in Welsh hotels are now very different, however one would have some difficulty in finding full board at under £3.00 per day or beer at 20p per pint which is the modern equivalent of what Bingley paid. Although now, as one suspects then, the warmth of the welcome tends to be inversely proportional to the tariff charged.

Indeed that sentiment was implied in an 1891 guide book, speaking of "cottage lodgings" – *"The Welsh housewife though perhaps not quite a paragon of neatness in her domestic arrangements, is, generally speaking, a liberal and sedulous caterer for the requirements of her visitors and takes a personal pride in their comfort, which one often misses in more sophisticated places"*.

Aside from the neatness libel, this is certainly still true of Welsh Guest Houses.

Apart from better accommodation modern walkers can now, in case of trouble, depend on the Aberdyfi Outward Bound Mountain Search and Rescue Team, although they will lack the companionship of legendary guides such as Robin Edwards and Richard Pugh. He will also lack refreshment at the summit hut that Pugh built, but still he will endorse H.P. Whynham's sentiments of Cadair –

"Few objects can be more awfully sublime than Cader Idris".

DYFI

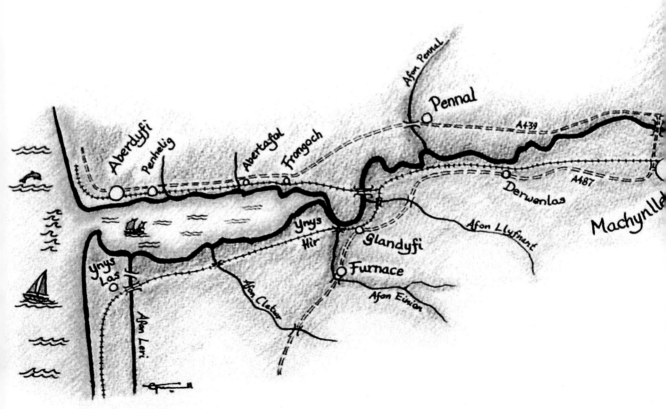

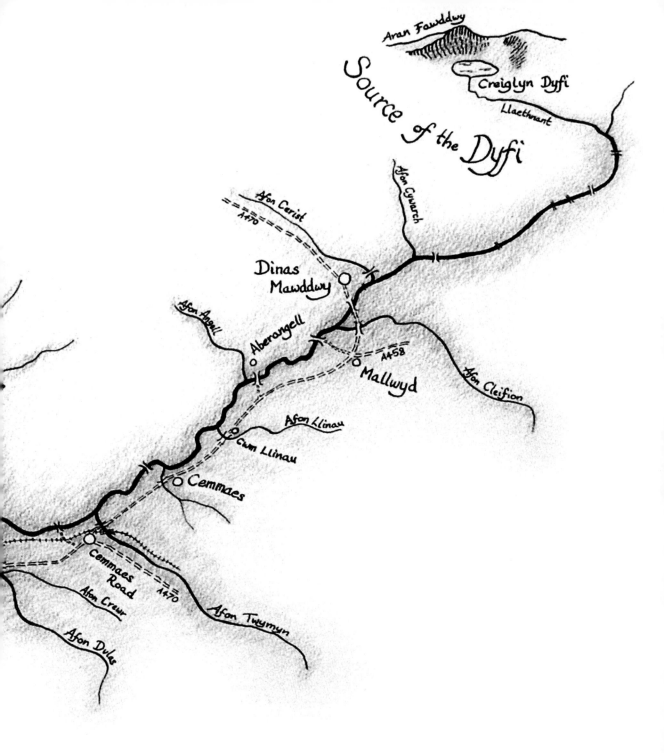

Source of the Dyfi

Aran Fawddwy

Creiglyn Dyfi

Llaethnant

Afon Cerist
A470

Afon Cywarch

Dinas Mawddwy

Afon Angell

Aberangell

A458

Mallwyd

Afon Cleifion

Afon Llinau

Cwm Llinau

Cemmaes

Cemmaes Road
A470

Afon Creur

Afon Twymyn

Afon Dulas

DYFI

1

THE SOURCE

Whereas the Mawddach bubbles idly from an undistinguished amorphous bog, the Dyfi is born of the lake Creiglyn Dyfi where buzzard and kestrel glide above semi-alpine flora.

Aran Faddwy, down whose craggy flanks the stream crashes, just fails to reach the magic 3000 feet, yet out-tops every other sub-Snowdonia peak. Even its better-publicised neighbour, Cadair Idris is shy of it by some forty-five feet and it towers above the vaunted Pumlumon by over five hundred. Indeed in the 1720s Daniel Defoe described the "Tovy" as *"Rising among the impassable mountains"*.

Unlike today's booted and knapsacked townies, local people did not venture into these heights, except for shepherding or other pressing necessity. Consequently such places became redolent of myth often with a suspicion of satanic associations, hence the old calumny that the Welsh were *"Devil worshippers"*. In fact Welsh people have always been conscious of the risks of a beelzebubian encounter, which is why in Wales place names such as "Devil's Bridge" or "Devil's Staircase" are eschewed for fear that Satan will claim them as his own. Indeed a stranger was liable to have his extremities scanned lest boots or gloves concealed cloven hooves and his backside surreptitiously eyed for any protuberance that might hint at the presence of a tail. Indeed this may have been the reason for the suspicion that William Hutton met in 1783 in the Dyfi valley. *" I stood single, the people eyed me as a phenomenon with countenances mixed with fear and inquiry. Perhaps they took me for an inspector of taxes, they could not take me for a window peeper as there were scarcely any to peep through and the few I saw were shattered and no glazier in the place."*

The youthful Dyfi protects itself from infernal interference by masquerading as the Llaethnant (milk stream) in memory of its waters being turned to milk by St. Tydecho a brother of St. Cadfan. They lived in the 6th century, times known in England as the "Dark Ages", but in Wales as the "Age of Saints". Indeed Wales was a country of saints, of the three patron saints of mainland Britain, only St. David was native to his patroncy, furthermore there are those who claim that St. Patrick was Welsh. Thus, when St. Augustine came over at the end of the 6th century supposedly to convert Britain, Welsh Christians could well ask, "What kept you?"

Despite having a past awash with holy persons and having at least half a dozen major indigenous denominations, Welsh people are uneasy with over-structured worship, hence the pre-eminence of the Annibynwyr (Independents or Congregationalists). But regardless of sect, no title is as respected even in these secularised times, as *Parchedig* (Reverend) except possibly *Bardd* (Poet). Of course anyone entitled to both designations enjoys a quite unassailable status.

Not pausing for such introspection, the Dyfi merges with a dozen brooks as it drops dramatically like a hawk on an incautious vole in a score of waterfalls and cataracts.

Unlike the rackety passage of the youthful Mawddach and its tributaries, thrusting like apocalyptic horsemen, the Dyfi assembles its allies in conspiratorial conclaves until it is ready to emerge in responsible sedateness.

Having thrown in its lot with the teeming Rhiwiech, the river emerges from hiding to reach Llanymaddwy, its first village. Here, on the church font soldiers allegedly sharpened their swords before the battle of Bwlch y Groes, that great watershed where an inch decided whether the Dyfi, the Dee or the Severn would be enriched by a drop of a warrior's blood. In this church, the old custom of Plygain is still observed, where the Christmas Eve midnight service, lit by a multitude of candles, is prolonged to dawn with singing and processions.

Like most of the starker regions of mid-Wales, agriculture was at subsistence levels in a barter economy based on produce swapping and domestic manufacture. William Thomas was still producing hand-made wooden hay rakes with traditional riven ash tines here at Llanymawddwy in the mid 20th century. Vital was the mutual interdependence, still manifest at harvests and sheep gatherings. However, tractors render unnecessary the pooling of oxen to make up the yokes of up to six pairs which were needed to pull the primitive ploughs on the heavy tilth of the tiny valley-floor holdings.

Although oxen were weaker than horses and had a useful life of a mere seven years, they could plough all day on a cud of grass as opposed to the oats needed by horses every whipstitch and, when their time came, instead of the fellmonger's few shillings, the ox provided leather, horn and meat in abundance.

As far as the really high ground was concerned, prior to the 13th century introduction of hardy sheep breeds such as the Merino, little was produced save billhook-gathered oats, coppiced wood for charcoal burning and peat sledged down from the mountaintop turbary pits.

Whereas the Mawddach is an "in your face, what you see is what you get", sort of river, the Dyfi abounds with excitingly hidden valleys. Afon Pumryd, (the "river of the five fords") in Cwm Dyniewyd, minor streams like the Lygoed, the Serfel and the Efailfach as well as the Cywarch, its lead mine concealed as if its existence was a state secret. These all hurry to unite with the Dyfi at Abercywarch, a tiny settlement, but not so tiny that it could not sire Elis Wynne, the great 17th century divine and writer.

Then the Dyfi makes its first major alliance with the Cerist and its fine and fertile valley and adopts its sedate and measured pace as its role model.

Further on, it is augmented by the Angell, with its tributary the Mynach redolent of monastic influence, having slate workings in a valley totally impenetrable until the coming of the clanking horse-drawn railway; as well as modest outpourings of the likes of Cwm Ddu, Blaen y Cwm and a host of other quiet unadvertised nooks.

Lower down again, the Dyfi is joined by the two Dulas'. The one coming in from the north passing through a convoluted valley of slate is overt enough but it is fed by tributaries in sub-valleys that are as covert as they come. In contrast, the mountain-born southern Dulas decisively knife-slices its way from the remotest recesses of Wales' central massif to once power every sort of mill at the village of Forge, the workshop of Machynlleth.

Strangers find it curious, although perhaps Machynlletheans would not, that there should be two rivers named Dulas confluencing at their town from opposite directions. Apparently having no commonality except the "blue/black" appearance implied by their shared name, but in fact these two opposing rivers were part of the same south east to north-west drainage pattern that was captured by the Dyfi, perhaps a hundred million years ago.

Unlike the Mawddach at Llanelltyd, the Dyfi at Llyn Bwrti the lowest of its 30 practicable crossing points, does not immediately break out into estuarial majesty but like a foal released from its stable, it makes some tentative twists and gambols before galloping into the full, exciting tidal world.

DYFI
2
DINAS MAWDDWY

Despite a miniscule population, its dignity of being classed as a "Dinas", i.e. a city with all its trappings of Mayor, Aldermen, Recorder, Burgesses with their Mace and Standard Measures, was a matter of great pride to Dinas Mawddwy. To enforce his powers, the Mayor had the Whipping Post and *Feg Fawr* or stocks. The Recorder had local jurisdiction over civil disputes of less than 40/- (£2), cases being pleaded by attorneys (i.e. any literate persons) who could charge a fee of up to half a crown (12.5p).

Since all this derived from a 14th century charter issued somewhat challengeably by the Lord of the Manor, it has remained in some ways a "Johnnie-come-lately sort of place. It lacks both a church and parochial status, remaining ecclesiastically an appendage of neighbouring Mallwyd, a distinction in name baffling to anyone with dyslexic tendencies.

The "City's" importance derived from being a meeting point of routes. Here the traveller up-valley has the choice of swinging left along the Afon Cerist and on over Bwlch Oerddrws into the Wnion valley and hence to Dolgellau the commercial capital of Meirionnydd. Or, he can stick with the Dyfi and go via Llanymawddwy to brave the bleakness of Bwlch y Groes pass, described by Pennant as the, *"Most terrible in North Wales to reach the summit where the cross stood to excite the thanksgiving of travellers for having so well accomplished their arduous journey"*. This route would take him to Y Bala, the emotional capital of Meirionnydd, a town whose standing is emphasised in Welsh by its definite article prefix.

Despite its city dignity, John Loveday in 1732 spoke of Mawddwy as *"Some houses built of hurdles and mud, thatched with fern with turf on ye roof ridge"* (Dinas is still a renowned place for ferns). Pennant some 70 years later considered that Dinas' *"One street of houses ill accorded a city."* Borrow was even more disapproving calling *"The collection of filthy huts, a dirty squalid place",* yet had these travellers been there in the 15th or 16th centuries rather than the 18th and 19th their strictures would have been more severe since it was then the abode of the *"Gwylltiaid Cochion Mawddwy"*, the Red Men of Mawddwy, whose red hair and heavy features were allegedly a throwback to pre-Celtic peoples. They probably were in fact disaffected "de-mobs" from the Wars of Roses, forced into this rural ghetto by a combination of economics and apartheid, a lack of both indigenous resources and recreational facilities inclining them towards robbery and rape.

Whoever they were, the royal writ failed to run, and a traveller venturesome enough to enter this "no-go area" might well be murdered for his bootlaces. Local residents lodged scythes and billhooks in their chimneys to prevent circumvention of their stoutly barred doors and oak shuttered windows.

On All Hallows Eve in 1555, having been pursued by a posse led by John Wynn of Gwydir and Lewis Owen, Vice-Chamberlain and Baron of the Exchequer of Caernarfon; 80 of the bandits "received their just deserts" (i.e. were hanged).

The mother of two of them vowed vengeance. Baring her breasts she called to Lewis Owen *"These breasts have given suck to those that shall wash their hands in your blood"*. In due course at a place now called Llidiart y Barwn (Baron's Gate, on the Welshpool road), Owen died with thirty arrows in him and it is said that brothers of the hanged pair "cut open the body and washed their hands in his blood".

Later, crime became "white collar" when fraudulent mine promotions replaced crimes against the person with crimes against the pocket. One of the more imaginative scams was the 1870s *Red Dragon Gold Mine*. This was run by an eponymous company with a prestigious London address that, besides holding the lease of this reputedly rich digging, had the rights to a machine which by a patented process allegedly converted ore into

gold. In fact all the backers possessed was an abandoned barren trial tunnel.

Potential investors were brought in by train, lavishly lodged and spirituously entertained at the Buckley Arms then, deeply inebriated, they were coached along the convolutions of the Sieglen valley. At its end they would find rock being trammed from an adit to a small building. Sworn to secrecy they would be allowed inside where they would see ore being tipped into a tastefully finished, brass-bound wooden box some 8'cube, inside which water-powered machinery ground and groaned. From a chute at the side a stream of what appeared to be gold particles emerged.

The punters needed little encouragement to *"Take advantage of this unique investment opportunity"*.

Isolated though this corner of Wales had been at the beginning of the 19th century, it could not escape the recruitment to fight Napoleon. Communities had to provide one man chosen by lot, but the man chosen was rejected and one Lewis Griffiths was ordered to take his place. Originally stationed in Ireland Griffiths' girlfriend followed, married him and accompanied him to Waterloo where she tended to his wounds. Griffiths survived to die in an accident at Braichgoch quarry, Corris in 1847.

Despite an 1851 population of a mere 288, there were 9 shoemakers and an astonishing 13 tailors. Although there was no church, there were 12 places of worship of other denominations, a total that is less surprising than it might seem since local splits might result in half a dozen denominations each having "a chapel to go to and one never to be seen dead in". This total could well be doubled if there was a requirement to have services in English, thus by the end of the 19th century quite trifling conurbations had pew space for half a county.

In Dinas what does sound excessive is the staggering total of 16 pubs and alehouses; with that amount of praying and drinking thus implied, it is a wonder anyone had time to go to work. Yet work they did and hard, almost all in weaving and agriculture. Not that all work was manual, Sir William Roberts who occupied Bryn Hall after Sir Edmund Buckley's death, made bacteriological discoveries in the 1890s that may have anticipated Fleming's work on Penicillin.

Breaking out into the flood plain, the river assumes a tranquillity that belies its earlier wildness. Anglesey apart, some of the best grain fields in northern Wales were here on the banks of the middle Dyfi, but yields were curtailed by lack of good lime. It was only in the 1830s that road improvements enabled distribution to be pioneered by the Dyfi Valley Coal and Lime Company of Richard Jones whose son John Jones became a noted bard.

Before the mid-19th century, coal would have been unknown outside the demesnes of the high and the mighty, peat turf being the universal domestic fuel. It was of course never bought, in fact to buy bread, meat or turf was considered to be the acts of a spendthrift. Turf was gathered at first near hearth and home and then as handy sources became exhausted successively dug higher and higher up the mountainsides. Patches of derelict land in places such as Cwm Cywarch mark diggings whose exhaustion forced turf gatherers to higher ground.

It is said that, in future, nations will battle over fuel, but in the past peat digging gave rise to much local acrimony or worse, in fact this may be the derivation of the term "Turf Wars". Under cover of darkness or remoteness, peat was dug and spirited away without the formality of lease or licence. Stacks of turf drying for winter needs, despite being guarded like jewels would shrink to non-existence on successive nights, since like hunger, cold cannot afford the luxury of conscience.

As regards other extractive industries, Dinas Mawddwy found itself on the periphery of the deposits that brought relative prosperity to neighbouring areas. Lead, copper, iron and later gold occurrences were tantalisingly just beyond reach, and the rich Ordovician slate veins that crossed southern Meirionnydd were stumbling to their last gasp by the time Dinas was reached.

Nevertheless, in the 1830s, with railways such as the Great Welsh Junction seemingly planning to thunder through the valley in their dash for Ireland, there was renewed interest in mining. Even as late as 1850 the £30,000 *Cwm Cowarch Lead Mine Company* was floated with 6 men being recorded as in work the next year. There were at least trials for metals in Cwm Dyniewyd and on Nant Lledfron and other tributary streams, and vestiges of an incline mark an attempt at slate working in Cwm Cywarch. The name of this valley, flax in Welsh, may indicate the growing of that crop in the distant past.

Indeed, the prospect of being virtually trackside may have spurred the founding of the vicinity's one successful extractive enterprise, the Minllyn slate quarry. Developed out of ancient digging, it was highly innovative, pioneering methods that larger undertakings not only eagerly adopted but for whose invention they claimed credit. Although main line trains never passed this way, from 1867 it did have its own private Mawddwy Railway. This $6^3/_4$ mile line, unlike other slate-dedicated lines was a full scale, standard gauge railway which, but independent, functioned as a branch of the Cambrian Railways, although, sensibly its planned extension to Llanuwchllyn via a $1^1/_2$ mile tunnel through the Aran massif, was never attempted. Despite also carrying slate from the Angell valley, the Mawddwy Railway was heavily subsidised by the landowner Sir Edmund Buckley of Bryn Hall.

Beyond the terminus station, now a private house, is the Meirion Mill where for a number years traditional Welsh woollens were woven in mills set up by a farmers co-operative *Y Gymdeithas Wlân* in the abandoned sheds of the quarry.

The last survivor of almost a score of the valley's wool related enterprises, *Y Meirion*, continues to flourish, but sadly it does so merely as a retailer of fabrics produced who knows where.

Here, still existing alongside its modern replacement is Pont Minllyn, built in 1533, it was for a century and a half the lowest stone bridge on the Dyfi. Opposite is the street of houses put up by Buckley as an intended extension to the main street of Dinas proper.

The next settlement is Mallwyd, a tiny hamlet that, like its parochially dependent near-namesake, is at a confluence of routes. Here Afon Cleifion provides a connection to England equally useful to Norman conqueror or Tudor usurper. It was the home of Dr. John Davies the 17th century divine and "Learned Druid", who contributed to Bishop Morgan's Welsh Bible and also, in 1632, complied the first Welsh dictionary that remains a standard work of reference for etymologists.

A little lower is Aberangell where in the latter 19th century terminated the little, clanking, horse-drawn Hendre Ddu railway that reached into the furthest recesses of the arboreal Angell valley serving slate quarries and farmsteads, as well as transporting timber in two world wars.

Having added Afon Angell to its inventory, the Dyfi continues to gather tributaries with the dedication of a train spotter. The Coegen at Cemmaes and the Twymyn at Glan Twymyn (or Cemmaes Road), that middle-of-nowhere rail halt that became a village in its own right.

Thus augmented, the Dyfi majestically sweeps on to Machynlleth where Henry, the fifth Marquis of Londonderry, tiring of his corduroy-breeched water-bailiffs being outwitted by the local salmon poachers, presented the fishing rights to the whole community.

DYFI
3
MACHYNLLETH

Allegedly the Maglona of the Romans, Machynlleth was a *Ne Plus Ultra* at the very limit of the Powis Marcher Lordship. It was seized by Owain Glyndŵr to isolate the inland Maldwyn territory from its maritime lifeline and where, if legend and the Welsh Tourist Board is to be believed, he established the first "Parliament for Wales", although one is assured that the mildly risqué graffiti scratched on slate in the garden of "Parliament House" are not attributable to him.

In what is now known as Royal House, Owain imprisoned his would-be assassin David Gam who later fought and died at Agincourt with the forebears of the Royal Welch Fusiliers whose traditions are maintained in the town by a detachment of the 7th (TA) Battalion.

Henry, Earl of Richmond, paused here to rest and to water his men and horses at Gariswn Well on his way to Bosworth field to win the day and seize the crown of England, without even providing Richard III with the horse for which he offered his kingdom.

Here at Gariswn Street were drilled the 9 Horsemen, 53 *pykemen* (armed with the throwing lance for which north Wales men were renowned), 18 *Harquebusiers* (pistol men), 13 Archers and 13 *Bylmen* (billhook men) of the Machynlleth Garrison raised and deployed to protect the dignity and person of Good Queen Bess. However, when in the Civil War drill was replaced by actualité, this gallant company of *Fencibles* proved no match for Cromwell's men who overran the town, burning many houses.

This pyromania arose from the fleeing Charles I finding shelter here, with the name Royal House defining his alleged hiding place. This tradition was later stoutly defended by Col. Ruck of Esgair Hall who claimed possession of the actual bed the fugitive monarch slept in. True or not Machynlleth, unlike Dolgellau, was stoutly Royalist, indeed even today a Cavalier flamboyantly striding, twirling his mustachios and doffing his hat to the ladies with extravagant gesture, would seem less out of place in Machynlleth than he would at Dolgellau from where the dour Calvinistic cloud has never been entirely lifted.

With the Restoration came reconstruction, a stone bridge being built in 1681 to replace the rather makeshift 16th century wooden structure. Its 1805 rebuild to facilitate the mail coach's passage still well serves modern HGVs.

Despite this Royalist adherence, Glyndŵr's insurgency remained dormant rather than dead, for in the 1830s Hugh Lewis the town's distinguished lawyer was a Covenanter supporter who hastened south to defend the "Children of Rebecca" arraigned at Carmarthen Assize for destroying tollgates.

If Dolgellau is a town for hard-nosed trading, Machynlleth commerce is more leisurely, where a quiet handshake seals a deal on a load of wool, a cow with calf to heel, or a pen of sheep at a market that has been held every Wednesday for three quarters of a millennium.

Besides livestock, timber and tanbark, Machynlleth had slate. In the course of five centuries it handled and traded in the produce of the quarries of the Dyfi, Angell and Dulas valleys. This industry spawned a need for cranes and waterwheels, weighing machines and tram wagons; a need that was met by the Rock Foundry, an innovative firm that in 1890 patented a *"Machine to facilitate the washing of clothes and household linen"*.

Trading has not always gone smoothly. In 1613 the drapers of Shrewsbury learning that "bootlegged" wool was being pack-horsed to Aberdyfi for export to France in contravention of their Royal monopoly, appealed to the Privy Council of King James I. His majesty having so recently lost 30,000 trees to the iron smelters of Dolgellau was excessively upset and took vigorous steps to identify the culprits, rumoured (correctly) to be

Machynlleth weavers. Not only were they never caught but their actions demonstrated that the Shrewsbury monopoly was unenforceable and in 1624 Parliament declared the markets open to all, although it was many years before the influence of the Shrewsbury drapers was finally broken.

By the 1780s the Machynlleth district was flourishing, labourers totalled 66 forming the largest employment group, but at 42 the weavers outnumbered the 38 farmers. There were 24 carpenters of whom 10 described themselves as ship's carpenters. There were 9 skinners, 5 timber merchants and the same number of slaters (a term which then embraced any sort of slate worker). There were 4 each of saddlers, tanners, masons, and blacksmiths, with coopers and glaziers each numbering just 3. There were 2 representatives for such diverse trades as card makers (the wood and brass combs for untangling raw wool), curriers, millers, hatters, butchers, attorneys, mariners and excise men (one being the pioneering publisher Titus Evans who was an excise man as a "day job"). Whilst singletons claimed to be barber, breeches maker, writer, bailiff, fuller, supervisor (of what?), stay maker, fisherman, harpist, watchmaker, forge man, fowler, miner, brick maker and parish clerk. As regards the last named it was part of his duties each Saturday evening to spread fresh rushes on the earthen floor of the parish church.

Of the retail trades there was just the one corn merchant and one flour merchant, with 8 being unspecified "shopkeepers".

There were 7 tailors but an astonishing 38 shoemakers, many of the latter would be occupied with mending boots and shoes rather than making them but it does show that at a time when many countrywomen went barefoot, Machynlleth must have been a "Mini Northampton" supplying footwear to a wide area.

There were just 7 who claimed to be "Gentlemen", but the number admitting to be innkeepers was a mere

5, an incredibly small number for a market town, although the "retailers of beer" were not listed; a degree of sobriety entirely unknown in Dolgellau is indicated. There were also 4 wheelwrights, equalling the number of blacksmiths, giving the lie to the assertion that up to the end of the 18th century wheeled vehicles were scarce in these parts.

Machynlleth had and still has Maengwyn Street where the Sergeant-at-Mace policed the market, charging each buyer and each seller a penny. It was here in 1798 that travellers stiffly descended from the very first mail coach to reach the town and stamped their chilled feet as they sought refreshment at the Unicorn. A pub later sycophantly named after the landowning Williams Wynns of Wynnstay. These bemused, "stage-lagged" voyagers would have found a town suffering from the rigours of Napoleaonic wars and the effects of successive bad harvests where, barely two years before, the Militia had faced food rioters.

By 1835 things were moving, although according to Pigot's directory the number of blacksmiths was unaltered, there were now 6 wheelwrights and 10 taverns, augmented by a dozen retailers of beer. The town being able to support 7 each of milliners and tailors, 2 watchmakers and 2 hairdressers is indicative of increased prosperity. The 6 butchers indicate that more meat was being eaten and the ability to afford candles instead of rush lights is evidenced by the 4 tallow chandlers.

Unfortunately a big decline in the stocking trade was looming on the horizon and the knitters would soon be reduced to hawking their wares to stagecoach travellers.

The town still comprised just three streets, Pentre-rhyden and Pentre-rallt intersecting Maengwyn Street with geometrical exactitude at the Town Hall, a building Bingley wrote of as being *"A Plain unadorned structure"*. He did however describe the town as *"Much more regularly built than most in Wales"* which, compared with Dolgellau which he had just left, was fair comment.

This regularity is partly due to the fact that although there were influential landowners such as the Vaughans associated with Dolgellau, none were omnipotently dominant as were the Edwards/Londonderrys of Machynlleth.

Maengwyn street, perfectly proportioned, a poor man's version of St.Petersburg's Nevsky Prospekt, still seems stalked by the spirit of Mary Cornelia, Nain Londonderry, who ruled the length and breadth of the valley and who made Plas Machynlleth a 19th century bed and breakfast for the crowned heads of Europe.

It was she who accompanied her husband, the fifth Marquis, to Russia by carriage (in winter!) to persuade his friend Tsar Alexander II to abandon his Balkan ambitions to lay Welsh rail-lines throughout his empire and modernise his industries by putting Welshmen in charge of them.

It was she who in 1873 built the Castlereagh clock of Tremadog stone, that stands at the street's end like a giant point-duty policeman, to mark the 21st birthday of the eldest of her sons, the old town hall being demolished to make way for it.

It was he, Henry Londonderry, great-uncle of Winston Churchill, who sponsored David Davies' breakthrough at Talerddig to carry the railway to the coast bringing prosperity to the region but ultimately taking the life of his second son in the crash at Abermule.

The railway-driven prosperity came not only from the communication facility itself, but also from the scores of footplate men, guards, cleaners, clerks, porters, drayman, signalmen and platelayers that it demanded, swelling the population by a third. Most of the new jobs were filled by incomers which did little to ease the plight of the dozen weavers, 5 yarn makers, and sundry tailors, tanners, curriers, covisors, tawers and other practitioners of forgotten trades, put out of business, their wares displaced by rail-borne manufactures. Somehow a tannery survived until 1880 and John Jones' Felingerrig loom was still working in 1910 although by the 1900s most wool was going to the north of England to fetch better prices than the local weavers and knitters could pay.

One of Machynlleth's many chapels, Maengwyn Street Welsh Presbyterian Church, was an unexpected beneficiary of the railway. David Davies was careful to balance dig with fill in laying out his railways, however at Talerddig what was planned as a summit tunnel had to be made into an exceptionally deep cutting. This created a surplus of stone, some of which was generously made available for the church's construction.

In Maengwyn Street was a tenement known as "The Barracks" which, as the 1881 census recorded, was a microcosm of the town, with occupations listed as; ostler, farm labourer, quarryman, miner, post boy, cash annuitant, woollen spinner, charwoman, tailor, lead mine chandler and collier (charcoal burner?).

Although it had at its peak almost a score of flannel makers, half a dozen yarn makers and a similar number of fullers, Machynlleth was not really an industrial town; the Dyfi's pace was too turgid to provide the flow demanded by trip-hammers and millstones so these, and the overflow of weavers and fullers, were located a mile out of town at Forge on the (southern) Afon Dulas. The name derives from the forge recorded

here in 1797 that was supplied with iron from the ironworks at Eglwysfach. This same stream later powered the district's first electricity station.

George Borrow in 1854 thought Machynlleth *"a thoroughly Welsh town with a stately church and one or two good streets, where the ancient British language is spoken with great purity"*. Later Beatrix Potter was less favourable, describing it as *"A wretched town where hardly anyone speaks English, with the Lion Inn a 'singular place'"*, but reserving her worst strictures for the railway, calling it *"past description, taking 4 hours to travel 60 miles"* a tardiness she attributed to *"the guard alighting to pick mushrooms"*. Perhaps Borrow was wise to walk.

Today following many changes of fortune Plas Machynlleth, née the Greenfield house and park of Sir John Edwards, is a fine municipal amenity. It was Sir John who having inherited wealth had the good sense not only to marry a rich lady, but on being widowed to marry an even richer one. It was his "coming out" settlement on his daughter Mary Cornelia that made her such a catch for a young Guards officer, who would unexpectedly inherit most of a couple of counties and a Marquisate. But in the end almost unimaginable wealth could not protect her from early widowhood or from the sadness of burying three of her children.

Not all wealth was inherited, Machynlleth boys who "made it big" included Owen Owen who opened his first Liverpool store aged 21 and the Wiggins, with their shops and paper mills. On the other hand wealth was no bar to other success, Berta Ruck daughter of the Easgair Rucks made her mark in 20th century literature.

The magnificent church gates, the pride of Machynlleth, were made at Shrewsbury by George Lloyd in 1843. Unfortunately for him renovations of the 14th century church were causing cash-flow problems, thus he had to accept £4 and a pig in settlement of his £9 bill.

The town's more curious buildings include the smithy whose frontage was hastily rebuilt in a horseshoe shape in 1896 by the, then, Dowager Marchioness since the old frontage was considered too tatty for the eyes of that connoisseur of frontages, the Prince of Wales, the future Edward VII.

Bereft of smithies and indeed almost any other industry, Machynlleth now takes on a "Green" aspect, with the nearby Centre for Alternative Technology and the new Dyfi bridge for the long-distance cycle track, besides capitalising on its history at the Celtica Centre.

However, the gem of modern Machynlleth is Y Tabernacl which the energies and enterprise of local people have made a centre of international repute for music and the arts, and host to the great Annual Music Festival. Thus is continued the Dyfi bardic tradition of poets such as Llywarch Hen (7th C) and Hywel Swrdwal (15th C), as well as that of artists such as Richard Wilson who in the 18th century first made Welsh people aware of their landscape.

DYFI
4
DERWEN-LAS

Just as Rome has its Ostia, Athens its Piraeus and indeed Dolgellau its Llanelltyd, Machynlleth had its Derwen-las, enabling it to stand aloof from the rough trades of stevedoring and shipbuilding. In its turn the nucleus of the village at Pentre Nant kept itself well apart from the docks and smithy on one side and the limekilns on the other. Up to 1834 it was something of a dead end since, until the coast road was built, travellers from Machynlleth to Aberystwyth had to strike inland via Glaspwll.

General supplies and limestone for the village's and other kilns were landed here but the main trade was outward, traditionally mainly agricultural produce and woollens. From at least the 16th century these were augmented by slate from Aberllefenni, Corris, Dinas Mawddwy and nearby Morben. Later, as the demand for lead for pewter mugs and platters grew, ores were brought over the mountain from Dyliffe and elsewhere. In fact Derwen-las became very much a lead port, the lead connection being reinforced when Catherine, a daughter of the Williams family, prominent in port affairs, married the lead entrepreneur, William Cobden of "Repeal of the Corn Laws" fame.

Like Llanelltyd on the Mawddach, Derwen-las was at the limit of navigation of the Dyfi and like Llanelltyd much of its trade was in barges of various types with trans-shipment at the river mouth, in this case at Aberdyfi. With its extensive Montgomeryshire hinterland it was much bigger than Llanelltyd and its slate and ore traffic made it more industrial in aspect. These products of quarry and mine did much to offset the loss of hinterland trade when the Montgomeryshire Canal reached Newtown in 1821.

Like Llanelltyd, ships were built here but on a larger scale. During the "Golden Century" of Welsh shipbuilding (1780-1880) 36 vessels were launched plus a score at nearby Morben, Llyn Bwtri. Garreg (Glandyfi) and Llugwy.

It was at Derwen-las itself that the great shipwright John Jones had a yard as did Richard Lewis. Most of their builds were sailing ships, stout little sloops and schooners, handy enough to run a creek in an onshore wind and strong enough to ride an ocean storm. In the 1860s, the "Quarry Maid" was launched, powered by a steam engine built by De Winton's, the great Caernarfon engineers, to the order of Col. Robert Davies Pryce, quarry owner and innovative entrepreneur.

From 1859 the port was served by the *Corris, Machynlleth & River Dovey Tramroad* which terminated at its subsidiary shipping point, Quay Ward, where its slate and lead warehouses and offices still stand as indeed does the Morben Magazine where black powder for the quarries and mines was stored.

In most Welsh townships, even at the revivalist peak, taverns and alehouses outnumbered chapels. Not so at Derwen-las, Tafarn Isa and Tafarn Ucha (now the Black Lion), faced a formidable line up of Wesleyan, Calvinistic and Congregational chapels, backed up by a Church and a Mission Hall, which collectively could seat a substantial percentage of the population of western Montgomeryshire.

Downstream is the little ore port of Morben where John Evans built his ships and, at the bend in the river, Llyn Bwrti was used by John Jones when his Derwen-las yard was jammed with keels.

By 1847 the various wharves were exporting 500 tons of tanbark, 40,000 feet of timber, 150,000 pit-props, 1500 tons of slates and possibly 500-700 tons of lead ore, and taking in 5,000 quarters of corn, 100 tons of coal, 2000 tons of limestone, 11,000 hides and sundry goods to the value of £14,000.

Much tanbark was produced at Morben by John Evans, some was shipped out but most went to the Machynlleth tanneries, the high tannin content of this Welsh tanbark and the good tallow from mountain sheep contributing to the quality of Welsh leather.

To make tanbark, gangs of women and children would strip spring-felled trees of their bark which was then stored under cover until the end of the felling season when the men would take over the cleaning of the bark, ready for sending it to the tanneries. Evans also hired out horses, having two teams each of 3 men and 3 horses.

1860 was the very apogee of Derwen-las' prosperity; the tram road was bringing in slate from Corris in tonnages that grew almost weekly, making this the world's most important slate port outside of Caernarfonshire. In addition, lead was booming and work was started on tram road extensions to serve John Evans' and John Jones' shipyards with a talk of pushing a further mile to Garreg (Glandyfi) where vessels of up to 700 tons could lie. As a longer-term project, a whole new non tide-dependant wharf at Glandyfi was envisaged.

Then, in 1862 disaster struck, in the form of Thomas Savin, the ubiquitous entrepreneur. In building his Aberystwyth & Welch Coast Railway, he not only robbed Derwen-las of its raison d'etre but also in a spirit of "You won't be needing this anymore", diverted the river, leaving Derwen-las on a land-locked ox-bow lake.

There is a certain wry amusement in the sequel to this action that killed the port stone dead. Shortly afterwards, like many rich people who recklessly seek to become even richer, Savin came seriously unstuck. The Dyfi showed its displeasure at its disturbance by attacking and eroding the grounds of the Llugwy estate of R.C.Anwyl, one of the protagonists of the A&WCR and later director of its successor the, Cambrian Railways. The Cambrian had the expensive task of trying to control the erosion by piling stones and redundant barges onto the bank to protect his mansion but the river responded by

attacking the opposite, southern, bank necessitating a long and costly wall which in no way helped the Cambrian's parlous finances.

Probably the most remarkable happening at Quay Ward was in 1883 when John Rees a Machynlleth watchmaker, suffering competition from factory-made timepieces, decided to diversify. He bought a boat and with the help of Graigfach foundry at Machynlleth, converted it into one of the world's first submarines! Not realising that Captain Richards was a mine captain not a mariner, Rees invited him to accompany him on the test dive. Richards possibly having suicidal inclinations following the closure of his Morben slate quarry some years before, agreed.. The vessel submerged as indeed submarines are intended to do, but it failed to rise. Fortunately it was close enough to the bank for the large assemblage of bystanders to drag it ashore with ropes and release the occupants.

At Derwen-las today, road improvements speed up the traffic, a camera-enforced limit slows it down. This contradiction seems to epitomise its search for a role that in a century and a half has emptied and closed its chapels and the pubs in equal measure, confined its commercial activities to a machinery yard and a caravan site, and seemingly contributed to the village's unique quality of glowering mystery.

DYFI
5
PENNAL

It was here in 1406 that Owain ap Gruffudd Fychan (Aka Owain Glyndŵr), writing in the Latin lingua franca of the day, exhorted King Charles VI of France to extend to Wales the same courtesies of co-operation against the English that his nation habitually extended to Scotland. He set this out in his *Pennal Letter* which was a sort of "Business Plan" defining his policy which included universities in both north and south Wales, an independent Welsh church under its own Archbishop and an Assembly; objectives that were only achieved almost five centuries later. In return he offered allegiance to the "Avignon" Pope, Benedict XIII. Unfortunately, although Charles sent a goodwill delegation, the military assistance consisted of one sword of a design more ceremonial that practical.

Although Glyndŵr has long been a focus of nationalistic initiatives and his name hijacked by *Meibion Glyndŵr,* the 1980s protest movement, Glyndŵr himself was neither hairy revolutionary nor jingoistic bigot but a respectable land-owning *uchelwr* (gentleman). Although his power base was Harlech Castle and his "capital" Machynlleth, his emotional epicentre was Pennal with the church acting as his own Welsh "Chapel Royal".

Long before Glyndŵr's day, the Llys on Domen Las at Plas Talgarth made Pennal a place of some significance. Its 6th century church has the dedication unique to Wales of "St.Peter ad Vicula" (St Peter in chains, Acts *XII*). Founded by the Brittany Saints Tannwg and Eithrias, it has links with the Chapel Royal in the Tower of London and also with the Syrian Orthodox Church and the monastery of St.Peter Jerusalem, the site of the "Upper Room" of the Last Supper. The church's oval "Llan" enclosure suggests the probability that it was a pre-Christian site. Once a daughter church of Tywyn, it has long been an independent parish that once extended as far as Corris. The churchyard has been remodelled and in 2004 part was imaginatively laid out as a tribute to Owain that includes a fine statue.

The first known residents were the Romans who established Cefn Caer which they may or may not have called Maglona. Little detail of this fort was known until 2000 when a magnetometry survey revealed details of it and its defences. The survey confirmed the line of the road running eastwards from the fort which was previously known only from cropmarks in aerial photographs and also showed ribbon development to either side of both roads leading from the main gates of the fort extending for over 220 yards (200m) beyond the defences. Various features were identified in the immediate environs of the fort including a bath-house, a circular tomb or perhaps a shrine, what appears to be a *mansio* or imperial posting station and other buildings, including traces of an adjacent parade-ground.

It was here where the Romans and many before and since crossed the Dyfi. Not that it was ever possible to do so dry shod but, within living memory, horse carts and driven cattle continued to come over from Quay Ward at low tide, the drivers and drovers preparing for or recuperating from the dangers and perils of the crossing at one of the several inns.

This ford, the lowest on the river, conferred considerable importance on Pennal but its primacy was wrested by Machynlleth in the 15th century when its bridge was built. Despite this some ferry facilities from Glandyfi survived into the 20th century.

Pennal became something of an outstation of Machynlleth flannel manufacturing but as the highest navigable point on the north bank, its Llyn Bwtri wharf remained a landing place for supplies and a loading point for produce for transhipment at Aberdyfi. There was some shipbuilding nearby at Llugwy and doubtless men also found work at the shipyards across the river.

The output of the Bryneglwys slate quarries was bought over the mountain by pack animal to be loaded

into small boats to taken down river to Aberdyfi. At the same time men from Pennal walked to work in the quarry, barracking there from Monday to Saturday. This trade was lost when the Talyllyn Railway was built but it was replaced by the output of local quarries such as Cwm Ebol from where a rail line to the river was built in 1868 which enabled slate slabs to be taken along the coast to factories at Aberystwyth.

A mere $1^{1}/_{2}$ miles long and horse/gravity driven, the Cwm Ebol line barely qualifies as one of the "Great Little Trains of Wales" but it is notable since it was the very last railed route ever laid in Wales to carry slate to a shipping point rather than to a main line railway. This slate traffic ceased around the end of the 19th century but the line continued for a time serving a small quartz digging.

Some of the land hereabouts was owned by Plas Talgarth, (built by Humphrey Edwards in the 17th century), and much of the rest by Pennal Towers which was occupied by the Thurstons a distinguished military family related to the Edwards, but the real movers and shakers were the extensive and influential Anwyl family. Their Tudor Llugwy Hall still survives in a riverside setting as fine as any in Wales, although actually much of the present structure dates from the 1890s after the Anwyls left.

The decline of Pennal was hastened by the lack of a main-line railway but this was not for want of trying. Well before what became the Cambrian Coast line was laid down in the 1860s, there were a number of railway proposals that would have involved a railway along the north bank of the river. The first, the 1850 *Aberdovey Railway*, would have run from Mr. Pryce's quarries at Aberllefenni through Pennal, but presumably, due to the daunting tunnelling involved, stopping short of Aberdyfi at Fron Goch. It was to have included a branch to the river at Ynys giving a deeper water alternative to Derwen-las. Such a line would, besides

handling the Abergynolwyn and Cwm Ebol slate, have benefitted a couple of slate diggings on the Thurston's' land. There were several subsequent ideas which would have extended the line to Aberdyfi and even to Tywyn.

In the event, these local proposals were overtaken by Savin pushing his line along the south side of the river. When the viaducting of the estuary failed and an inland bridge point had to be selected, there was much to recommend a crossing upstream of Pennal but Glandyfi proved a more expedient location.

In 2004 Pennal became, with Machynlleth, the focus of the sexacentennial of the Glyndŵr Parliament and his being crowned Owain IV. The commemorative sword, a replica of Glyndŵr's specially forged to mark the occasion, ought perhaps to have remained in Pennal but Machynlleth's superior political muscle won the day.

Beyond Pennal, towards Cwrt, where the old road strikes over the hill for Tywyn, the Lancastrians under Thomas ap Nicholas fought and beat the Yorkists of Harri ap Gwilym. Harri and many of his followers were killed; Harri himself being buried near the gate of Escairweddan farm. His men were interred along the road thereafter known as Wtra'r Bedddau (*Lane of Graves*); a Dolmen in a field nearby allegedly commemorates them.

DYFI
6
GLANDYFI, FURNACE, YNYS HIR

Here at Glandyfi (*neé* Garreg) where the river, the road and the railway jostle for a share of the miniscule coastal strip, only the solitary stationmaster's house remains of the once bustling railway station. The goods yard, where clanking slate and lead ore carts converged and fresh-caught salmon was rushed to market, is now a green sward but of the shipyard and landing stage nothing remains. So effectively have all traces of maritime activity been erased that it might have been dismissed as legend had not a soil sample, anomaly found in the late 1990s some 2m below the surface of the erstwhile goods yard, indicated the site of a landing stage.

A footpath leads a few hundred yards to the new Glandyfi station which is a little unmanned halt, the sad successor to that Crewe of Wales, Dyfi Junction. It was hastily constructed in isolation on a bleak bog when the river was bridged following the abandonment of the plans for an estuary viaduct. Although these plans envisaged only a simple junction (facing from Machynlleth) this was a full triangle very much like the Mawddach arrangements.

At this busy station travellers to and from English destinations cosmopolitanly mingled with those from Gwynedd and Glamorgan, it being alleged that if one tarried there long enough one would meet all the great and the good of Wales, as well as an appreciable proportion of the bad and the ugly.

David Lloyd George paced the platform on his way to meet world leaders or, it is alleged, crouched in impromptu incognito en-route to adulterous assignations. It is suggested that the notion of his revolutionary "Old Age Stamps" (to provide pensions) came to him here whilst stranded by a missed connection.

However, tarrying was generally not popular in this bog-built structure since discomfort apart, subsidence was a constant anxiety, passengers invariably fearing that if their connections were unduly delayed the whole shebang would have vanished into the morass by the time it arrived. Chilled by the biting wind huddled over a waiting room fire in a fellowship of shared adversity, chance meetings must have resulted in many a deal being struck, plans devised, friendships made and romances sparked. Less happy was the lot of the staff, composed almost exclusively of men who had incurred the most extreme displeasure of the honchos of the Cambrian Railways, and suffered exile to this Cymric Siberia.

It was of course purely an interchange and to or from which a ticket could not be bought. It is said that since junctions were shown in the same large type as towns (such as Newtown or Aberystwyth) on the Cambrian Railways publicity maps, sample-case impeded commercial travellers would attempt to alight at this apparently important conurbation.

Although even in its heyday the Junction comprised only a small group of structures, it sprawled over three counties. The north end was in Montgomeryshire, the south in Cardiganshire and the bridge keeper's house, technically part of the station, in Meirionnydd. The bridge keeper was there to ensure the prompt operation of the opening section of the bridge whenever a ship wished to pass.

This was a somewhat rare event since the railway construction robbed Derwen-las of its water and Quay Ward of its traffic so the bridge-keeper must have must spent many lonely hours in his cabin awaiting the telegraph signal that would summon him to his levers.

Immediately to the west of the erstwhile Glandyfi station the road jibes to the left and the coast to the right, leaving the railway bereft of companionship to strike across an extensive coastal flat passing Domen Las, the

mound of a motte & bailey castle at the mouth of the Einion.

Just along is the village of Eglwysfach where, at the church of St. Michael, R.S. Thomas, the darkly brooding unofficial poet laureate of Wales ministered for 13 years from 1954 and wrote some of his finest work.

During the Civil War, when the Parliamentary forces were threatening Aberystwyth, the Royal Mint in that town was relocated here at a silver smelter. John Ray writing in 1658 describes *"Four great wheels whose turning guides the rising and falling of the bellows and stampers."* It is believed that there were five furnaces and a stamping mill in addition to the mint house. The name *Furnace* survives from the time when it was the chief industrial village of Ceredigion.

In 1693 Sir Carberry Prys claimed to be loading at Glandyfi the lead and silver ores produced by 600 miners. Buildings and walls hereabouts of alien stone brought in as ballast are the sole reminders of this £90,000 pa (£8.5 million today) enterprise.

In 1755 the Einon River that had powered the smeltery was used for a blast furnace that, despite the lack of success of earlier furnaces further north, was built to meet the inexorable military demand for iron in the build up to the Seven Years War. Such furnaces required charcoal, creating a voracious demand for wood which, outgrowing the capacities of coppices, denuded landscapes of standing timber.

This deeply offended the Lords of Admiralty, whose seamen might proverbially be of iron, but whose ships were still of wood, so that furnace masters and their insatiable wood-gathering charcoal burners tended to be hounded out of the Naval regions of the south and east of England. Thus, although iron ore had to be brought

down from Cumberland, this site was chosen due to the availability of wood.

The scale of wood requirements is shown by the size of the charcoal warehouse that dwarfs the furnace (now restored following its use as a sawmill). Apart from the need to keep charcoal dry, a building was also needed to shield it from prying eyes since an ironmaster known to be low on fuel would soon find himself paying over the odds in order to keep his furnace in blast. Also the store needed to be secure since it was rumoured that charcoal burners were not above supplying charcoal stolen from a furnace's own stockpile.

Wood was always the limiting factor on production and even with supplies coming from as far as the upper Towy valley, this huge warehouse was soon emptied and wood shortage undoubtedly contributed to its 1814 closure.

Lead mines flourished up to the 19th century producing besides silver, some copper and zinc. The nearest mine, Ystrad Einon, had an almost unique 16' raising and pumping water wheel located underground. More elaborate was Bryndyfi mine with its tramway, ranges of buildings, copious machinery, every adjunct to efficient operation and 100-strong payroll; it only lacked one thing – metallic ores! More successful was the Glandyfi slate quarry which produced slabs for the enamelling works at Aberystwyth. The Einon valley now devoid of almost all traces of industry, provides under the name "Artists' Valley" a most picturesque route towards the heights of Moel y Llyn.

In earlier times great mackerel fleets sailed this stretch of river under their elected "Admiral". In fact well into

the 20th century during the June to September season, half a dozen or more boats each with 3 crews each of 3 or 4 men would cast nets for salmon and sewin round the clock. They lodged in huts on the marshes with unattached men sharing on the hot bed principle. Some men would have families with them, the wives and children gathering mushrooms which, with the fish, would be rushed by rail to Midlands markets.

Sadly just 3 boats are now licensed and they operate very much on a hobby basis.

Now with all these various activities long gone, the "chief industry" is the fine RSPB Ynyshir Reserve. Centred on Long Island, which indeed was an island among the marshland, it is adjacent to Ynyshir Hall, the 17th century seat of initially the Lloyd and then the Knolls families.

On more than 1000 acres of peat bog, salt marsh, reed beds, pools and woodland, (partly 16th century shipwright's oak) are to be seen the likes of Greenland white fronted geese, widgeon, pintail, mallard, teal, shoveller, shellback and other species. Moths, butterflies and dragonflies are to be found and, in season, snowdrops, bluebells, anemones and other flora.

Quite apart from nature and wildlife, and indeed the scenery and landscape, reserves such as these provide a most enhancing refuge from the noise and rush of life that is becoming increasingly urbocentric.

DYFI
7
ABERTAFOL

Fron Goch, today a tent factory and boating centre, was the site of a small, but fully mechanised slate quarry. Despite the railway cutting right through its site, it remained faithful to water transport. A tunnel under the road and railway brought slate blocks from a pit-working to a steam-driven mill nestling against the shore side of the railway embankment as if sheltering from the elements. The finished product was trammed out along the little jetty for shipment to Aberdyfi, coal for the boiler coming in as a return cargo. Built to its present form in the early 1870's, it closed when the jetty was damaged in the terrible winter of 1883/84 and, in the slump conditions of the time, a rebuild could not be afforded. The delightful group of buildings, in part having an appearance more ecclesiastical than industrial, still survive.

A little beyond is Pant Eidal where holidaymakers provide a steadier income than its trifling scratching for slate ever could.

Beyond again is Abertafol whose most prominent edifice is a telephone box but its stream, Afon Tafol, provides a footpath to the treeless elevated hinterland, Llyn Barfog ('bearded' lake) and on to the mines of Cwm Maethlon and the old Cwt-Tywyn turnpike. Once a popular walk, Bwlch farm on the saddle above the Cwm used to provide teas to thirsty hikers.

The Cwt-Tywyn road actually provides easier access to Llyn Barfog, the abode of that horrifying monster, the *Afanc*, which terrorised the surrounding countryside for generations. No one knows exactly what the *Afanc* looked like; it has been variously described as a dragon, a crocodile, or even a particularly fierce variety of beaver. All efforts to kill the monster only resulted in fruitless loss of life until one day the problem was heard of in Camelot, whereupon King Arthur mounted his mighty horse *Llamrai* and galloped to the rescue.

He succeeded in getting a rope around the beast, dragging it out of the water in a somewhat cowboy fashion and dispatched it with his sword *Excalibur*. Such was the effort involved in landing the creature that the horse's hoofs dug into the rock leaving an indentation visible to this day in a stone known as *Carn March Arthur* (Stone of Arthur's stallion).

Actually the truth is more prosaic, it was not a monster who struck terror but the Irish who, in post-Roman times established an unwelcome presence here and indeed a sheepfold close to the lake is said to denote the site of one of the three churches that the Irish built in the area. Also nearby tumuli are traditionally called the *Irish Graves* and a small stone circle is called the *Irish Church*. The Arthurian allegation may well have arisen from the seeking of out-of-area help in tackling the incomers.

Less well known is the story of the three sisters whom being elderly and unmarried were inevitably called witches. They farmed nearby and had Welsh White cattle a breed that still survives hereabouts. One day one of the cows, Meinwen by name, wandered off to Dyffryn Gwyn where the farmer instead of returning it, mingled her with his own herd. The sisters missing their cow called to her by name, whereupon the entire Dyffryn Gwyn herd answered the call. Meinwen rejoined her herd but in accordance with their witch-like ways, the sisters put a spell on the neighbour's cows causing them to vanish into Llyn Barfog.

Cattle, particularly hill cattle, always answered the farmer's call if they suspected he might be bringing feed and it was not unknown for a beast to answer a stranger's call. However any vanishing was more likely to be to the abattoir or the mart rather than a lake!

Legend apart, this was the land of self-sufficiency, of farming folk who if they couldn't make it did without

it. Bread was home-baked from their own corn carried on their backs to the miller, or even hand-ground on the quornstone. Butter was made in a churn that, if one was lucky, was dog powered. Peat fires were charged from gathered turf; hay-rakes, spades, tableware, even the plough itself were all made from osiers or fallen trees. Dairy vessels were laboriously chiselled out from solid blocks of stone and clothes were made of cloth they had spun and woven, possibly from wool scraps gathered from hedgerows.

Such people had no use for money - which is just as well since they didn't have any!

Living from harvest to harvest, famine always hung like a Damoclean sword over these communities. Hunger could drive men to a desperation that overcame innate honesty. There was a long-standing myth that during the great famine of 1547 the occupant of Trefri Fawr, fearing pillage, took the oats from his barn and stored them in the roof-space of the house. The truth of this tale was proved over 400 years later when, during renovations, large quantities of near-fossilised oats were found lodged in the structure.

Not that four centuries is considered a particularly long time in these parts when properties have been in the same family for much of that time and many of the demesnes listed by Edward I in 1291 are still occupied.

This is *hafoding* territory where the whole ménage, beasts and all, would up sticks on *Calan Mai* (1st May) and head for the hills where they would live on the *hafod* until *Calan Gaef* (All Saints Day, November 1st) carrying on with all the routine tasks, cutting fodder, digging peat, tending stock, baking and making butter and cheese. This practice seems to date from around the 14th century when the climate became markedly colder discouraging winter living at higher locations.

The dwelling would be the *hafodty* – the summerhouse, not a garden gazebo, but a simple house, traditionally circular in emulation of a Celtic hut and usually situated in a sheltered nook by a stream. By the late 18th century, the dwellings were somewhat more elaborate, Pennant describing them as *"A long low room with a hole in the roof at one end to let out the smoke from the fire beneath. Their furniture is very simple, stones for stools and beds of hay."*

Actually, by Pennant's time, most *hafodtai* would be somewhat more salubrious with fireplaces, chimneys and rudimentary furniture, although not all would have had glass in the windows. In any case with hill farming concentrating on sheep and store cattle confined by stone walls rather than dairy herds, the need for these migrations was already diminishing

Some of these dwellings would have been *"Tai Unos"* (one-night houses) where, according to custom, if a house could be built between dusk and dawn and have a fire burning in the hearth, tenure was automatic. There was never any legal basis for this and whilst landowners were unlikely to enforce removal, a ground rent was liable to levied. The original house would have been very simple indeed and replacement by a more permanent erection would soon follow, thus anything now extant is unlikely to be part of the original structure.

Sometimes the older members of the family remained below in the *hendre* , "the old house", with just the younger ones spending the summer on the *hafod*. This could be a popular arrangement since it provided them with a temporary escape from the strictures of both their consanguine elders as well as the chapel elders, leaving them free to engage in such activities as "bundling" without the bundle. In a one-roomed cottage in winter with the family hogging the seats round the fire, a courting couple would lie on the bed but the young woman's mother saw to it that she was tightly "bundled" to prevent any untoward contact and with said mother keeping an eye and an ear on things, scope for mischief was limited.

Inevitably "accidents" did occur but in a society where families were dependent on children's economic contribution, pre-nuptial proof of fecundity was a wise precaution. Even when no wedding ensued, illegitimacy tended to be regarded generously, with the child being readily accepted into the family, its only stigma being possible relegation to the junior end of the sibling pecking order.

It is interesting that Dwynwen, the 5th century Saint and great aunt of St. David, whilst eschewing male contact herself, is represented as taking an understanding attitude to erotic frailties.

Such charitable attitudes were more typical of Welsh nonconformity than the rigid moral absolutes that grew up in the later 19th century largely as a defence against the Royal Commission Report of 1847 (The Blue Books) that branded the Welsh as intemperate and immoral.

Land enclosure and improvements, plus the milder climate of the 19th century, meant that some *hafotai* became year-round homesteads, but most were abandoned to collapse into today's scattered ruins. In a few instances, probably due to habit and a kind of holiday-home ethos, "hafoding" survived into the late 20th century.

High-grazing stock still has to be brought down in autumn either to winter on the farmer's lower ground or to be sent to a winter grazing contractor. Either way there is the spectacular sheep gather where all the neighbours pitch in to herd hundreds of beasts down to lower ground.

The steep, elevated slopes are rulered by the dry-stone walls whose construction from glacier-borne detritus cleared from the fields enriched no merchant or middleman and offered a lee in which a sheep might shelter from sun or storm. In the quite recent past it seemed that the art of dry-stone walling would die but thanks to various bodies such as the National Park this ancient skill is now being nurtured and encouraged.

It is on these slopes that transport became a challenge. Often even the two-wheeled sledge or the wheel-less slide car could not be used. The only possible conveyance for peat being the hand barrow, a bier-like frame carried by two men. Hay was gathered, near the farmstead at least, by dragging the cut hay with a looped burden rope.

Even in less hilly parts the tumbrel-sledge, essentially a box on runners, was used for manuring and liming which, since it carried its noxious cargo at a lower level than a wheeled cart, spreading was easier and less unpleasant.

Now the roost is ruled on the higher ground by the ubiquitous quad bike. Although some farmers still use a pony, the man on the quad bike with a bale of straw on the front carrier and a sheepdog in the rear box now epitomises Wales as firmly as the lamp-carrying miner once did.

DYFI
8
YNYS-LAS

Towards the extremity of the southern shore of the estuary, the levee-contained Cletwr joins the Dyfi where, in the 6th century among the reed beds, ancestors of the three now remaining Dyfi net fishermen effected a Moses-like rescue of the infant Taliesin, proto-poet of Wales. Elphin ap Gwyddno Garanhir, the owner of the fishing rights, took the lad home and found he could not only talk but also compose poetry of great beauty and complexity.

Legend has it that about this time one of the chieftains, Maelgwn Gwynedd, tiring of inter-tribal power struggles, persuaded his fellow chieftains to unite under the leadership of one of their number. It is alleged that they would all sit on their thrones at what is now called Traeth Maelgwn and, assuming none succeeded Canute-like in stemming the incoming tide, the last man left seated would be recognised as the *Tywysog Mawr* (the great prince) – since Maelgwn had a floating throne he won!

This chicanery serious eroded his popularity and when the infant Taliesin's prophesy of the downfall of Maelgwn proved correct, his reputation was made. Spending much time in north Wales, Taliesin is said to have gained inspiration from the tranquillity of Llyn Geirionydd, a tranquillity that speedboats now deny today's poets.

Near his foundling place at Tafarn Fach, (Little Tavern) renamed in the interests of sobriety and with an eye to the tourist trade as Tre Taliesin, is his reputed grave

Inland from here, where the main road crosses the Cletwr is Tre'r Ddôl, once known for its fulling mill and its lead mines (that in ancient times were also sources of copper) as well as its slate workings. No trace remains of its hat making, a mini industry that flourished at a time when a gentleman would almost as soon appear in public bare-buttocked as bare headed. Tre'r Ddôl's pub and café now make it of more renown as a place of refreshment.

On the very mouth of the Dyfi is the National Nature Reserve of dune and shore life. Besides the fauna and flora it has a fine wooden sculpture by Mick Petts that doubles as viewing platform and the centre's fine mosaic is a unique cooperation between artist Jenny Fell and community groups. Among the dunes live lizards, stoats, polecats, rabbits and voles and above them fly skylarks, meadow pippits and rare ringed plovers. From the boardwalks can be seen butterflies and moths, and flowers such as marsh and bee orchids.

At Ynys-las itself, is the mouth of the river Leri, like the Cletwr cunningly canalled in an 1820s reclamation scheme. This barren, windswept place, with its solitary 16th century Ynys Cottage (which still survives) elevated on the original Ynys (Island), would have been called in modern terms a "Ferry Port", the embarkation point for crossing the treacherous tides to Aberdyfi. Bishop Baldwin crossed here in the 12th century and Giraldus Cambrensis followed him in the 13th. By the 15th century a charge of 7/6 (35p) for a coach and 2d (1p) for a person on foot made it a nice little earner for the squires of Ynysmaengwyn; these fees being respectively the equivalent in modern terms of around £250 and £6. There were at one time three separate ferries crossing the estuary carrying passengers, livestock and wheeled vehicles respectively.

The area first came to national prominence in the time of Queen Elizabeth I. Due to the war with France salt had risen in price from at most 8d (3p) to as much as 2/6 (12.5p) per stone.

Realising what a burden that must be to her worthy subjects subsisting in winter on salted fish and meat, Good Queen Bess arranged for saltings to be set up in various places including the south side of the mouth of the Dyfi. Here the receding tides could be trapped and following natural evaporation, the residue could be boiled over peat fires to produce salt for a predicted 7d. At Tilbury she would shortly claim that she had the heart of man, but now she demonstrated that she also had the brain of an accountant since she proposed to sell the salt at the full 2/6!

When the opportunities for profit were realised there was a stampede of Dukes, Earls, assorted courtiers and sundry hangers on seeking a "piece of the action". This wrangling delayed matters for some 3 years, so production did not start until 1567. By this time the spat with France had abated and, amid all the furious salt-making activity on the shore at Traeth Maelgwn, a French ship cast anchor off Aberdyfi just across the river loaded with salt (and wine) to its groaning gunwales for which they were desperately seeking a buyer. Thus the whole ill-considered enterprise was abruptly ended.

In the early 1860s ex-draper Thomas Savin pressed forward vigorously with his grand scheme to enchain the whole of the Bae Ceredigion coast from Aberystwyth to the extremity of the Llŷn peninsular with railways and hotels.

On the Dyfi, in replication of the Mawddach layout, he envisaged a line along the south bank to a junction at the south end of a trans-estuary viaduct to the seaport on the north side.

Savin established a depot on the west bank of the canalised Leri at Ynys-las for the landing, storing and forwarding of everything from nails to rails that he needed to press his line southward to Aberystwyth, and to tranship similar supplies to Aberdyfi from where he was pushing his line north. This West Wharf was served by a branch of the main line that passed along the wharf, through the depot and on for $^1/_2$ mile to a deep-water wharf near the traditional ferry terminus.

Opposite on the eastern side of the Leri, and also rail connected, was his Penrhyn wharf. Initially planned to be 400' long, this size apparently arose from his intention of not only making "Aberleri" a seaside resort but also to usurp Aberdyfi's role as the main port for the Dyfi. The viaduct was to start from about $^1/_2$ mile east of here, running almost due north to Penhelig just east of Aberdyfi.

Temporary housing was built for the host of Irish navvies but as far as permanent housing was concerned, Savin only built half of one row before it sunk into the muddy reclaimed tilth! The story that the dwellings vanished from view with smoke coming out of the chimneys like a stricken liner slipping beneath the waves is an exaggeration, in fact most of the materials were salvaged and reused elsewhere.

Abandoning all hopes of a conurbation here, Savin concentrated his efforts on firmer ground further down the coast expanding the little village of Borth, then described as *"A picturesque hamlet of two rows of white-washed tenements with earth floors and thatched roofs"*. It eventually became a modestly successful seaside resort with a population that exceeded both Barmouth and Aberdyfi.

At the time though, Savin's enthusiasm ran ahead of reality trumpeting the possibilities that this new town offered. It is recorded that three gentlemen travelled down from London to investigate what business opportunities this booming resort might have to offer. Finding that the luxury hotel where they had reserved rooms just a building site, they were offered alternative accommodation on the straw-covered floor of a rail wagon. They bedded down in a siding at Borth but defective braking arrangements meant that they awoke some three miles downline at Bow Street. Actually when it was finished, the Cambrian (later Grand) Hotel was quite a fine place with an extensive kitchen garden growing produce both for hotel use and for sale via the railway. Before being demolished in 1966 it had latterly been Pantyfedwen, a hostel for Urdd Gobaith Cymru, the great Welsh youth organisation.

When Savin failed to find solid footings in the Dyfi's shifting sands for his trans-estuary viaduct, he planned an alternative crossing a little distance upstream where the riverbed seemed firmer. This "Plan B" would have

been a double-decker affair with a roadway underneath the railway, anticipating by some hundred and twenty years the arrangements (in reverse order) at the rebuilt Britannia bridge across Menai Strait. It had been hoped that the inclusion of a (tolled) road crossing would have attracted investment but that scheme was also not to be. The mouth of the Mawddach is formidable but it is a tranquil lake compared with the Dyfi's rip tides and Thomas Savin, that most gung-ho of railway builders, had to admit defeat.

Everything came to a halt in 1867 when, financially speaking, the wheels fell off all Savin's wagons. He found himself with pressing liabilities of £2.3 million (£106 million in early 21st century terms). This was more than covered by assets, which in modern terms totalled £160 million but, due to his practice of accepting shares in lieu of cash for his construction contracts, was almost entirely in unrealisable railway stock. He did escape ruin, but only just.

When the wreckage of Savin's collapsed empire was picked over, his successors abandoned the viaduct idea and crossed well upstream near where the Romans forded, thus creating Dyfi Junction and by dint of some nifty tunnelling reached Aberdyfi by the north bank.

The re-siting of the river crossing ensured that Ynys-las would never usurp Aberdyfi's role as the port of Dyfi so the grand extension of the Penrhyn Wharf was abandoned, the West Wharf line being retained to serve the ferry, appropriately renamed the *Aberdovey Ferry Branch*. Savin's sawmill on the east bank was revived in 1871 by Jones & Griffiths, the Aberdyfi timber merchants, who continued to use the Penrhyn siding. When they moved across to the west wharf in 1892, the disused *Aberdovey Ferry Branch* was re-laid and, confusingly, re-named the "Penrhyn branch"; both these siding/branches are traceable.

Borth remains as some kind of monument to Savin, it continues his seaside resort role coupled with that of

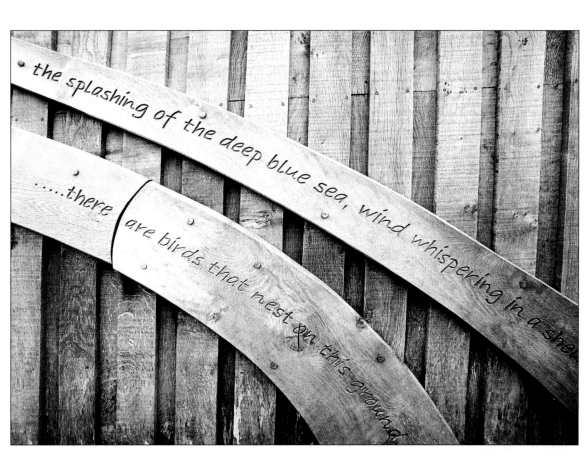

the splashing of the deep blue sea, wind whispering in a she...

.....there are birds that nest on this ground

a dormitory for Aberystwyth, but little of Savin's vision for Ynys-las came to fruition. House builders have found the firm ground on Ynys-las' dunes a little way away from Savin's ill chosen site; most are bungalows crouching low to dodge the howling equinoxial gales that the house agents doubtless describe as bracing breezes.

Although "Aberleri" as a town and port came to naught, the name is preserved by Messrs Steel-Kit who fortunately memorialise an ancient name as well as worthily upholding the Dyfi shipbuilding tradition. Although they use an old place name, their methods are strictly 21st century and one would search their premises in vain for adze or brace or steam-kettle let alone oak for frame or plank for clad.

Whilst building few complete vessels, they mainly produce, by computer-aided design, "flat packs" of steel components that can be readily transported to be welded together in remote locations even under very primitive conditions. Although aiming at a third-world market ,they have produced a number of small craft both for private and official users in the UK.

Their factory, built on the site of the 1892 sawmill, has turned out more vessels than all the traditional Dyfi yards put together ever did.

Maintaining the hi-tech mode of present day Ynys-las a fibre-optic cable from there now carries a thousand conversations and countless megabytes across the estuary to Aberdyfi.

DYFI
9
ABERDYFI

Aberdyfi was where ships were built, sailed and their captains schooled; where slate and other precious produce was exported, and even within living memory where Liverpool ships brought comestibles to the grocers, cloth to the tailors and sundry goods to every retailer in the town.

It is celebrated in song for its bells, but what bells? Since there was no church until the 1840s, which did not have bells until 1937, they were not church bells. There is a theory that when the "Mantua" was sunk in 1735, it remained relatively intact in shallow water and that the tide caused its ship's bell to emit a ghostly toll. There is a suggestion that it was due to the practice of belling sheep (the bellwether) but this ancient practice was too widespread to be identified with one place. There is a legend that a great tract of land including churches lies under Bae Ceredigion, the manifestations being the rock ridges of Sarn Bwch near Tywyn and Sarn Cynfelyn near Aberystwyth, as well as the vestiges of trees seen at low tide between Ynys-las and Borth. However, the possibly of a settlement inundated at the end of the Ice Age having a church is remote!

The Aberdyfi area was certainly populated in Neolithic times, as was proved by the finding of a stone axe 1985.

One of the earliest written records dates from the early 12th century when, aided by Richard, Bishop of London and King Henry 1st's steward, Cadwgan ap Bleddyn and his son Owen escaped from Ithel and Madog, sons of Rhirid ap Bleddyn by taking ship at Aberdyfi.

It was here in 1140 that north Wales Princes Owain Gwynedd and Cadwaladr invited Prince Anarawd ap Gruffudd ap Rhys, together with David, Bishop of St Davids and other clerics, to deplore the interference in Welsh Church affairs by the much junior, and by implication inferior, Church of Canterbury. Anarward's son Rhys built a castle here ten years later, but very shortly the Norman wrath descended in the form of Earl Robert de Clare, who unceremoniously destroyed it. Its mound is now prosaically known as Beacon Hill.

The first known maritime mention was in 1159 when an Irish ship apparently anchored off where Aberdyfi now stands, presumably in search of fresh water and there is also evidence that a ferry operated at this time.

Here some 50 years later, Llywelyn ap Iorwerth and the great and the good of Wales signed the "Treaty of Aberdyfi" legitimising Llywelyn's conquests and extending to Wales all the privileges of Magna Carta. This has been described as the first Welsh Parliament anticipating Owain by almost 200 years.

In 1560 there was reference to fishing for herring which, when salted, formed a major part of the Meirionnydd diet; but since Aberdyfi had only three houses, no boats were actually based there.

The real sensation of the 16th century was in November 1587 when a 120-ton Spanish caravel, the *Bear of Amsterdam,* dropped anchor in the estuary. The vessel remained there, an object of wonder and awe for several days until the gallant Merionethshire Militia, reinforced by their equally gallant friends of the Cardiganshire Militia, showed up to seize the warship in the name of the Queen. Unfortunately a suitable boat could not be found and being out of musket range, the artillery-less militiamen could only play a waiting game.

One morning at daybreak, the vessel was gone, never to be heard of again. In the meantime eight men had swum ashore, two were killed, four were captured and rumour has it that the missing two enjoyed a generous reception from the young women of the locality resulting in the Latin cast of countenance allegedly

to be seen in Aberdyfi to this day.

Although Aberdyfi was perceived as a poor relation of Barmouth, it had a Customs House in 1599 long before any other port on Bae Ceredigion and from the late 1500s trade began to develop with corn coming in from the Bristol Channel and salt and corn from Chester. By 1647 500 tons of ore per annum was being shipped to John Port, a lead factor of London in addition to tonnages to Bristol and elsewhere; a total that would multiply many fold by the end of the 17th century. In 1649 a captured Holdstein vessel loaded with corn was sent under escort to Aberdyfi to relieve famine. This escort being the first recorded "convoy" in what would later become the "Western Approaches".

During the 18th century shipping tonnages grew and the 1748 Admiralty Survey confirmed Aberdyfi as an official port, with cargoes of corn being regularly landed to feed a growing population. By this time the herring fleet numbered about 50 catching on a good night over a million fish. Most were sold outside the area but this intense fishing meant that there was a glut of other fish, including salmon, available to the local people at giveaway prices. Hence it being said that there were people so poor that they had to survive the winter on smoked salmon!

The oldest house in the town is Royal House on Seaview Terrace (built in 1614) and then known as Tŷ Mawr, it is where travellers stabled their horses and waited for the ferry. It was later named the Raven after the crest of the Corbets of Ynysmaengwyn. Later when a Stuart princess found herself benighted here, it was promoted to the style and status of the Royal Raven; it is now a shop.

Although the Corbets are more closely associated with Tywyn, their Aberdyfi influence was strong, they

built the Corbet Arms at Aberdyfi in 1775. It was intended as a coaching inn for the turnpike then being built from Machynlleth but, since the turnpike swerved inland at Cwrt to run direct to Tywyn, the inn had to wait until 1807 to greet its first "coach party", when the Corbet-built road from Cwrt was completed (vestiges of this road remain below the present road). Even then a regular coach service had to await the opening of the 1829 turnpike after which visitor numbers built up with hotels such as John Felix's Britannia and Hugh Edwards' Penhelig Arms being opened to serve them. The establishment of a Plymouth Brethren congregation in 1842 suggests that by then visitors were becoming residents and certainly the building of an English language Presbyterian Church in 1893 confirms that the "incomer" controversy is not a new thing. Features of most Welsh seaside towns are the elaborate chapels housing English-speaking congregations that were usually built by wealthy retirees from Lancashire and the Midlands.

In Aberdyfi the lack of ground meant that all denominations faced the same problem; the burial of the dead. Sometimes the coffins were hand-carried along the sands to the little burial ground a mile outside the town, others were carried by horse-bier to the chapel at Cwm Maethlon.

Keeping up with the times, the Corbet Arms was rebuilt to meet railway trade in 1867, but it burnt down in 1914 and a primary school now occupies its site. The present Dovey Hotel was built as the Ship Inn by Athelstan Corbet and several plaques around the town commemorate family members such as one that reads -

Anne Owen [neé Corbet]

Widow

A D

1733

The Corbets fell on hard times in 1878 but their estate was snapped up and the benevolence continued by a distant relative, John Corbett (SIC) of Droitwich. In a curious continuation of the Elizabethan salt saga at Ynys-las, Corbett had made a fortune in salt.

As an isolated, strictly maritime town living by fishing and by the transhipment of cargoes up and down the river, Derwen-las' mid 19th century boom reflected on Aberdyfi's fortunes, it being reported that at one time 80 vessels were seen on the river en route between the two places.

Vessels such as the 800-ton barque Glanlavon owned by Jones & Griffiths, the Machynlleth timber merchants, worked a transatlantic trade. Apart from slate, lead and various ores out and bricks, lime and general cargo in, ships on the Liverpool run regularly brought servant girls home for visits.

Aberdyfi also acted as a "Port of a port" for Tywyn. Since the Dysyni could only accept the tiniest of vessels, an attempt was made to build a pier (Pier Road being built to access it) but tide and storm defeated its completion. Thus Aberdyfi tended to handle Tywyn's sea borne trade and long before the Cambrian Coast line there were several proposals to rail link the two towns.

The railway came in 1867 when, following the failure of a direct viaduct, the re-aligned railway by dint of three tunnels (with Penhelig station jammed between two of them) somehow threaded its way though the narrow coastal strip giving it direct access from Machynlleth. Although the building of ships on the Dyfi did not cease until the 1880s, by the time the railway arrived it must have been in decline since rubble from tunnel driving obliterated a boatyard (forming Penhelig Park). Although the railway hit shipping activities, the port found a fresh role loading slate cargoes brought from the then furiously busy quarries, via the Corris, the Talyllyn and the Mawddwy railways.

Curiously one enterprise failed, namely the steam flour mill of 1881, since although such mills using steel rollers had made the old millstone mills obsolete, the flour trade was by that time moving to the big city mills. A similar mill near Tywyn was equally unsuccessful. Also unsuccessful was the 1889 attempt to provide a regular steam packet service to Waterford.

This apart, trade boomed, metal was mined and slate dug, in some cases virtually within the confines of the town (the former at the top of Copper Street, the latter at Penhelig). Intensified agriculture meant that lime and guano were also landed. A branch line to the beach with turntables to a two-level jetty enabled cargoes to be handled at all tides by a rail-mounted steam crane that doubled as a shunting engine.

With rail replacing droving there was much cattle traffic so the wharf included dockside pens. There was even a proposal to build a full-scale floating dock but bigger ships and the reduction of rail freight-charges stemmed such ambitions and the landlady replaced the longshoreman as the mainstay of the town.

Fishing became a speciality niche-market seeking lobster and crab, whilst the old sailing ships managed to find cargoes in the Mediterranean fruit trade. One odd maritime activity was that of the Elettra, the steam ship from which Marconi, in conjunction with his base at Tywyn, conducted experiments during WW1.

In the interwar years shipping languished, although Messrs David Jones' weekly steamer continued to arrive

with the groceries from Liverpool and two barques owned by local timber merchants sailed to the Baltic, making Aberdyfi the last port on Bae Ceredigion to have an overseas trade.

Being comparatively isolated, where in winter at least a stranger would be as noticeable as a naked ballet dancer, made the town ideal for covert war-time activities and in both world wars amphibious and other training went on. In WW2 the most bizarre function was the training of "Enemy" soldiers! Actually they were refugees from the Nazis but, because agents were believed to have been infiltrated amongst them, they had been interned. Released, they had scorned enlistment as Pioneers or other back-up troops, insisting on the most active of roles and in 1942 86 were trained here at Aberdyfi to form 3 Troop of 10 Commando.

A special bond grew up with the people of Aberdyfi and the survivors (23 were killed in the war) still visit commemorations at the memorial at Penhelig Park

Now the ten shipyards of Thomas Richards, Richard Roberts, Roger Lewis, William Williams, the ubiquitous John Jones and their like, where over 50 keels were put into the water are gone but the maritime tradition is upheld by Outward Bound whose 1941 foundation to provide young men with seamanship training was the precursor of many throughout the world.

The tradition is also maintained by the Rowing Club and their Celtic longboats, sturdy seagoing 4-oared craft modelled on pilot cutters, their League races are re-enactments of the one-time rush to claim a pilotage fee from an incoming ship. With no flash marina to attract the "gin and tonic navy", the members of the Sailing Club are real seamen, so too are the crew of the inshore lifeboat, adept at snatching the unwary from the unforgiving shoals, their state-of-the-art high-speed inflatable replaces a dynasty of lifeboats that since 1837 has played a big part in the life of the town.

Modern radar has rendered redundant the guide maker on Beacon Hill but the magnificent view from its bandstand remains. In the meantime, a sharp lookout over the town's affairs is kept by the Aberdyfi Griffin (or is it a Dragon?).

Oddly, golf looms large in the economics of the town. Founded by the redoubtable Col A.E.Ruck of Esgair; the club was the first in Wales and continues to attract many leading players and their attendant followers.

The Literary Institute that, as the inscription shows, was built by John Corbett in 1897 is still a delightful asset but the high spot of non-maritime Aberdyfi is the great August Parade which is led by local school children carrying hand-made lanterns.

List of Photographs - One

List of Photographs - Two

ACKNOWLEDGEMENTS

Over the three years it has taken to compile the photographs, and research the tales for this book, many people have helped Jean and Alun in a number of ways. Farmers have gladly given permission for Jean to cross their land, some have told us stories and others have lent precious, long out-of-print volumes. Jean has particularly appreciated those who have assisted her in carrying heavy photographic equipment over mountains and valleys. Alun in his wide travels has met nothing but kindness and a determination to assist. Both have made many new friends.

Ian Andrews
Sonja Benskin -Mesher
Barbara Bryan
Merfyn Wyn Tomos - Dolgellau Record Office
Crew of the Viking – Barmouth
Twm Elias
Elinor Evans – Dolgelynen Farm
Elwyn Evans and the staff of
    Dolgellau library
Don Fullerlove – Steelfab
Jack Grasse
Rev. Eirlys Gruffydd
Andy Hall -
    Arthog Outdoor Education Centre
Catherine Havard
Tony Hodgson
Gwen Hough
Shelagh Hourahane
Hugo Iffla
Rev. Geraint ap Iorwerth
Jon Isherwood
Andy Jeffrey – Outward Bound Aberdyfi
Danny Jones

Heulwen Jones
Phyll Jones
Richard Jones – Farmers' Mart Dolgellau
Ruth Lambert – Y Tabernacl
Leslie Leigh
Edward and Bethan Lewis
Machynlleth Library
Kevin McArdell – Oriel Barmouth
National Library of Wales
Rev. Aubrey Newell
Photo Imaging - Bangor
John Pinder
David Roberts - Trefrifawr
Peter Rowlands
Chris and Sally Shaw
Janet Simcox
Victoria Street –
    Meirion Mill Dinas Mawddwy
Graham Stringer
Harry Toland
Jane Whittle
Richard M. Williams
(The late) Sir Glanmor Williams

Special thanks to Chris Terrell for the excellent maps, Y Tabernacl Machynlleth for the use of their archives and to Myrddin ap Dafydd for his encouragement and Jim Perrin for his Foreword.
And last but not least Cati the Dog - Jean's photography assistant.